Edly's
Music Theory for Practical People

by
Ed Roseman

with illustrations and cover art by
Peter Reynolds

with layout and other graphic manipulations by
Edly

ISBN 0-9661616-0-2

Musical EdVentures™
106 Arundel Road • Kennebunkport, ME 04046-5206
(207) 967-5433 • fax: (419) 818-4688
www.edly.com e-mail: edly@edly.com

Contents

Notation Examples

Diagrams, Charts... Other Examples

Questions?

Ask Edly at http://www.edly.com

Prelude

To Students, Teachers, and Other Potential Readers

Do you play an instrument or sing—at any level, and want to know more about what makes music tick? Do you want to deepen your appreciation of music? Are you a rock 'n' roller who wants to broaden your horizons? Are you a jazzer needing more knowledge of the chords and scales which make up your music? Are you classically trained and wanting to branch into popular styles? Do you want to read from fake books?

If you answered yes to any of those questions, then this book is for you. It is intended for anyone, teen to adult, who wants to learn about what's going on *inside* music. It starts at the very beginning by introducing the notes and explaining basic terms. It then takes you through scale and chord building from simple to advanced. It introduces you to standard song forms, improvisation, and ear-training. After reading this book, you will have a very solid grounding in melody and harmony. At that point, if you wish, you can continue your study with books that focus on your specific areas of interest.

Throughout, I have tried to present the material clearly, informally, and even with some sense of humor (perish the thought) where possible. I hope this helps make the material more palatable and the reading more fun.

Why the title "Music Theory for Practical People"? The reason is that there is nothing *theoretical* about most music "theory"—especially that contained in this book. So-called music "theory" is concrete, immediately applicable, and... *practical.* Understanding music's patterns and formulas makes everything a musician does easier. Learning theory will help you become a better musician, regardless of your musical specialty. Learning theory is a very practical thing to do.

There *are* musicians who make wonderful music without having any analytical understanding of what it is that they are doing, or how the music they make is constructed. I strongly believe in the power of intuition in making music. I also believe that the combination of intuitive *and* analytical understanding is even more powerful. One need not rule the other; they work together, sharing the brain and musical ear.

In writing this book, I do not in any way hope to dictate how you make your music. Rather, I intend to begin to demystify the *structure* of music. I want to give you tools that you can use to understand the music that you and others make. I further hope that you will expand your ways of making music because of that understanding. While reading, I strongly encourage you to experiment with and *use* the material you are covering. The 'rules' in this book are merely descriptions of how things are conventionally done. Learn these conventions, but feel free—and even *invited*—to break any 'rule' in this book!

The musical language in this book is that of twentieth-century popular music—jazz, rock, and their various spinoffs. But be assured, although the language may be that of the vernacular, many of the concepts hold true over the ages and across styles. Therefore, a musician with previous classical theory training (harmony or counterpoint, etc.) will probably find some of this material familiar. Those moving in the other direction will find that classical theory will come more easily after reading this book. It's all connected, after all.

Throughout the book, each new topic comes with a packing slip with explanations of **what** it is, **why** it's important (and why a student should bother to learn it), and **how** it's made. More advanced topics also often include an explanation of **who** might find it helpful. Certain topics are revealed only gradually, encouraging you to participate more actively in the discovery process. There are workbook exercises scattered throughout the book. Have fun with them. Consider writing your answers in pencil, and fear not, the answers are in the back. Teachers, if you prefer to correct your students' work yourself, rip or cut out the answers.

Feel free to skip around the book. Read a chapter's introduction; skim the chapter, and then use your good judgment to decide if you want to skip ahead, rather than getting bogged down in something you don't immediately need. You can always come back.

Do-it-yourselfers: this book was written to stand on its own. You will learn *a lot* by snuggling up alone with the book. But a good teacher would be a great help in bringing some of the harder concepts to life and clearing up any problems you come across. Either way, good luck!

Finding Your Way Around in the Book

- Hey, everyone! This (૭) is the symbol I'll use when I have a special note for you. It will be something I want you to be sure to notice. Don't miss these, ok?!
- Words that are in the glossary are written in ***bold italics***. In this book, the glossary and index live together in the same apartment (take a look at pages 137–144). This way, you look things up in one place rather than two.
- Workbook problems and other such riddles answered in the answer section are indicated by a capital letter A impaled by a flat. (A)
- You'll know that a notation example is coming up soon when you see a treble clef (𝄞) embedded in the text.

About Reading Music... or Not

I believe that the ability to *read* music need *not* be a prerequisite to *understanding* music. This book was written to help players of all instruments, and singers—readers and non-readers alike—learn how music is put together. I must add, though, that our culture is so visually oriented that it is helpful to *see* what you *hear*. Musical notation accomplishes this beautifully. My bottom line is that *I encourage anyone who wants to become truly facile with music to learn to read.* Otherwise, even with outstanding ears, you will be cut off from the huge body of literature that exists in standard musical notation. I would hope that, after reading this book, even the previously most staunch non-reader would be convinced of the value of reading music… to the point of willingly committing to learning it.

After the preceding pro-reading pep talk, I'll say that *Edly's Music Theory for Practical People* does *not* attempt to teach you to read music. In contrast to learning theory, I think it's probably easier to learn to read music from a book devoted to just one instrument. Ask at your local sheet music store. If you want to learn to read music, though, let me strongly suggest that you do so *with the aid of a teacher*. The money you pay the teacher will save you so much frustration that you will be happier, though somewhat poorer. The investment will pay off in terms of the hair remaining on your head which you otherwise would have pulled out. It is a rare student who can teach himself or herself to read music.

Another thing: this book also doesn't deal much with *time* aspects of music—rhythm, meter, etc. I believe that *time* in music is best learned with the help of a teacher. Rhythm, counting, and meter need to be *demonstrated*, and are rarely learned well or correctly solely from a book. I strongly recommend finding a teacher for help with musical time.

For those who *do* read music, this book contains plenty of notation examples (marked with a treble clef '𝄞' in the text.) I've tried wherever possible to show examples both in standard notation *and* in plain English. Notation examples are both in treble and bass clef so as not to discriminate against people who only read bass clef. *However,* many—if not most—of the bass clef examples will sound muddy if played on the octave shown. These should be played on a higher octave. Trust your ear. If your ear isn't trustworthy, then *train it!* You'll have lots of help later in this book.

Business Stuff

- Edly's Music Theory for Practical People can be purchased at many music and book stores throughout the USA, or directly from Musical EdVentures™. E-mail or write for further info or to be put on the mailing list so I can let you know about upcoming releases. You're also invited to visit my website, where, among other things, I'll do my best to answer your questions in the "Ask Edly" column.

Musical EdVentures™
106 Arundel Road · Kennebunkport, ME 04046-5206
(207) 967-5433 · fax: (419) 818-4688
www.edly.com e-mail: edly@edly.com

Acknowledgements

Thanks to Coby Keller for her loving support, Greg Jalbert for his consistent inspiration, *Musical Ed* font, exploding piano player illustrations, and layout suggestions, Peter Reynolds for the rest of the illustrations, and Michael Hauser for the title. Thanks to Suzanne Boutilier for the photo.

Thanks also to all my editors and proofreaders, including Coby Keller, J.C. Conley, Byron and Ellen Roseman (hi, mom & dad), Daniel Fredgant, Tom Randall, Nancy 3., Carl Dimow, Brian Bender, Pauline Uyeda, Ross Galati, and the students who pointed out the—very, very few (!?)—typos. These people are definitely rated 𝄪 (double sharp—see below) in *my* book.

More thanks to all my teachers, especially to Betty Hanson for her multifaceted encouragement, Carl Rondina for beginning my ear-training, Jan Kryzwicki for sparking my interest in music history, and Jon Barlow for giving me a small glimpse of just how big the bigger picture really is. Finally, thanks to those of my students who are also my teachers, without whom I never would have written this book.

This book was written using MacWrite Pro™ by Claris on a Macintosh™ Centris 650 computer. Notation examples were created using Encore™, by Passport. The hand-lettering font is Brian Willson's wonderful *Marydale* font, available online.

Abbreviations

Standard Abbreviations and Symbols

+, aug	augmented
°, dim	diminished
ø, ø7	half diminished
𝄫	double flat
𝄪	double sharp
♭	flat
M, maj, Δ	major
m, –, min	minor
♮	natural
P	perfect
#	sharp
4, sus	suspended
TT	tritone
8ve	octave
8va	play an octave higher
unis	unison

Other Symbols Used in this Book

𝄞	see notation example
A	see the Answers section
☺	a special note from me to you

Edly's Quick Guide to Notation

Who? This little chapter is for those of you who already *read* music, and want to *write* music in standard notation. Actually, it's also for anyone who is going to attempt to read your manuscript—I've seen some manuscripts that I just *could not* decipher. The Quick Guide to Notation does not undertake to teach you to read music. It is meant to fill the gap between being a *reader* of music and a *writer* of music. Those of you who don't read music or will not be writing anything in standard notation can skip to the next chapter.

There are spelling rules and handwriting conventions in music just as there are in language. In both cases some of them seem very nit picky and others are obviously vital. If you're going to be writing much music at all, even *a half-hour* spent with a good "rules of manuscript" book will pay off immeasurably. Check at your local music store or music library. If you are writing music for a class, you'll get better grades (I hope) if your teacher can read what you actually *meant* to write. More important, musicians in the real world will actually be able to *read* what you write, and will therefore *play it better!* Not bad for curling up with a book for a half-hour. Okay, end of pep talk. In the meantime, here are some suggestions to help make your manuscript more legible. 𝄞

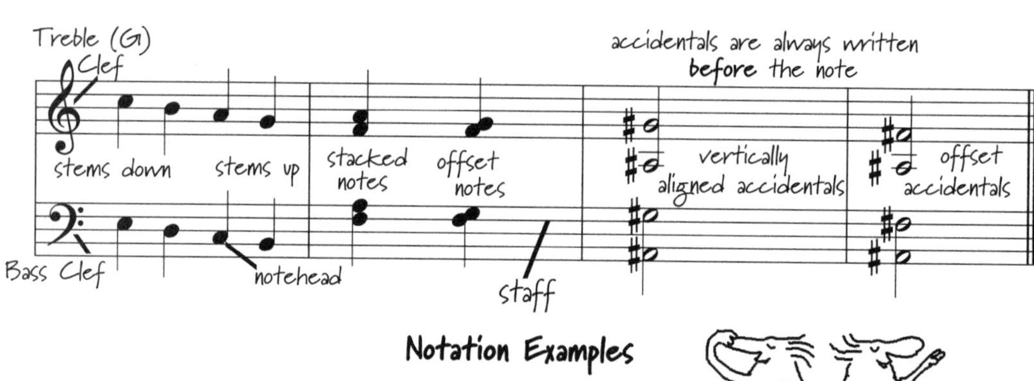

Notation Examples

Staff: The five lines upon which music is notated.

Clefs: *Do* include clefs! *Clef* means *key* in the sense of 'the key to a puzzle—or a door.' In this case, the puzzle is knowing what notes the lines and spaces represent. Even though the treble clef (𝄞) is the most common clef, bass clefs (𝄢) are people too! You'd hate for a wandering trombonist to happen upon your music and misread it, wouldn't you? (It happened to me once, and it was *not* a pleasant experience.)

Stem Direction: Stems of notes *on* or *above* the middle line of a staff are "stems-down." Notes lower than this are "stems-up." This keeps the stems inside the staff as much as possible, rather than above or below. Also, by the way, music is more legible when stems are truly vertical—straight up and down, rather than slanting. Honest. Also, stems are on the right for stems-up notes, and on the left for stems-down notes, as if you rotated the note 180° rather than just flipping it upside-down. See the notation example.

Stem Length: Stems extend one octave. In other words, if the note is a D, the stem extends to the D an octave in the correct direction.

Placement of Accidentals: (Sharps, flats, and naturals—as well as *double flats* (𝄫) and *double sharps* (𝄪), both of which you'll officially meet later—are all examples of ***accidentals***. They raise or lower notes' pitches.) Although we *say* and *write* (in text) the accidental *after* the note ("F sharp" or "F♯"), when notated on a staff, accidentals are written *before* the note, on the *same* line or space as the note they modify.

Offsets: The notes of a chord are normally stacked vertically. Two notes on adjacent lines and spaces are offset—one to each side of the stem. Accidentals on notes closer than three lines or spaces away are offset so they don't overlap.

Noteheads: Noteheads fill an entire space—from one line to the next! They are pretty sumptuous looking, when you get right down to it. Give your noteheads a fighting chance—don't make 'em scrawny!

Ledger Lines: Ledger lines are short lines that continue the staff higher or lower so notes beyond the staff are not floating in limbo. Their spacing is the same as that of the lines on the staff. Therefore, the first ledger line below a staff is the same distance from the staff's first line as is the staff's second line.

These few guidelines should be enough to make your manuscript legible. Here are some blank staves for some notation of your own.

Chapter 1~ The Musical Alphabets—Natural and Chromatic

The (Natural) Musical Alphabet

The musical alphabet has seven letters, A through G, as opposed to the English alphabet's twenty-six. Unlike the English alphabet, though, the musical alphabet has no real beginning or end. It goes forwards as it ascends: A, B, C, D, E, F, G, A, B, C, D, etc., and backwards as it descends: D, C, B, A, G, F, E, D, C, and so on. Notice that you can start on any note. These notes are all *natural* (♮), by the way, meaning neither sharp (♯) nor flat (♭).

Natural notes are only part of the story of the musical alphabet, though. Let's agree on some vocabulary so we can sanely discuss the *chromatic scale.*

Half-Steps, Whole-Steps, and Octaves

Pitch: ***Pitch*** is how high or low a note is. A *high note* is *high* in pitch, and a *low note* is *low* in pitch.

Half-steps: The distance from a note to the next closest note (regardless of whether either note is sharp, natural, or flat) is a ***half-step.***

Whole-steps: Two half-steps form a ***whole-step.*** Half-steps and whole-steps are the basic building blocks of all musical structures.

Octave: An ***octave***[1] is the distance from a note to the next higher or lower occurrence of that note, for example A to A, or E♭ to E♭. There are twelve half-steps in an octave. I hear you protest, "But 'oct' means eight, not twelve!" Ah, but we are both right. There are, sure enough, eight notes (A, B, C, D, E, F, G, A) in an octave, if you count only *one* occurrence (whether sharp, natural, or flat) of each *letter* of the musical alphabet.

1 Made you look! Want a more technical definition? Here it comes. The higher a note, the faster its sound wave vibrates. The lower a note, the slower it vibrates. Notes an octave apart vibrate in a ratio of 2:1. That is, a note vibrates twice as fast as the note an octave lower. For example, the A above middle C vibrates 440 times per second. The A below middle C vibrates 220 times per second.

On a piano, from any note to the *next closest* note (black *or* white key, whichever is closer) is a half-step. On fretted instruments such as the guitar, mandolin, or banjo, from one fret to the next (on the same string) is also a half-step. Take a look at the following diagram of the piano keyboard, guitar and mandolin fretboards, and violin fingerboard (fiddlers, ignore the frets). Only the natural notes are listed on the fretboards.

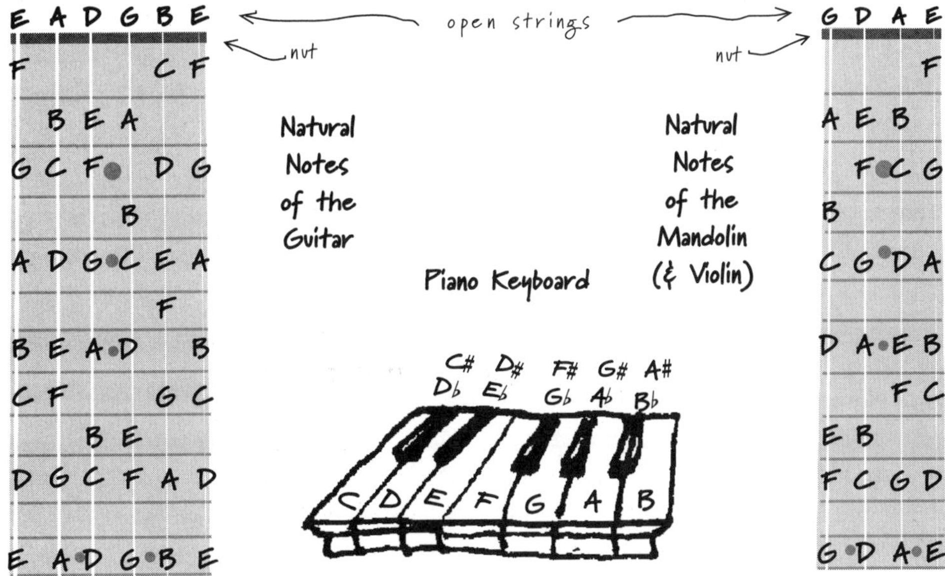

Guitar, Piano, & Mandolin (& Fretted Violin)

Notice that the pattern formed by these natural notes is *irregular* on all three instruments. On the guitar and mandolin, the pairs E and F and B and C are always only one fret away from each other, whereas all the other notes are two frets away from their closest neighbor. It turns out that the blank frets are sharp (or flat) notes.

You can see the same thing on the piano: every pair of white keys has a black key in between, again except between B and C, and between E and F. The white keys are natural notes, and the black keys are sharps and flats. This is how the piano got its zebra pattern of alternating groups of two and three black keys.

Regardless of instrument, adding the sharps and flats to the natural notes gives us the complete *chromatic alphabet*.

A *sharp* (♯) raises the pitch of a natural note by a half-step. A *flat* (♭) lowers the pitch of a natural note by a half-step. A *natural* (♮) cancels out a flat or sharp. Sharps, flats, and naturals—as well as *double flats* (𝄫) and *double sharps* (𝄪), both of which you'll officially meet later—are examples of ***accidentals***. *Accidentals* raise or lower notes' pitches.

Got all that? If not, take a deep breath and read it once more. Or read this: accidentals, like accidents, are something unexpected which happen to a note, as in: "Wall lookee heah; a shahp! I giss dat makes da note a half-step highah." Feel better now? Good.

The Importance of Scales: A Pep Talk

What is a scale?

How are scales made?

Good questions! A scale is a collection of notes in a specific pattern, beginning on a note *(the tonic)*, and ending on the same note an octave higher or lower (from A to A, or from C# to C#, for example). The type of scale dictates the pattern—or vice versa. Most scales consist of half-steps and whole-steps, although some scales also include ***intervals***[2] of a step-and-a-half. Fewer still include intervals of two whole-steps (or four half-steps), nestled somewhere within the scale.

Why learn about scales? Scales are important for many reasons. Melodies are made up of fragmented scales, and/or chords. Chords are derived from scales. Thinking in terms of scales gives a musician a bird's-eye view of music, making it easier to see the whole, rather than thinking of music as a succession of random notes. When you understand scales, you gain access to a system of thinking of notes in groups, instead of individually. The advantage is that you can package seven notes as *one unit* (a scale) instead of seven *separate* elements. That's seven times less information to keep track of! You might think of this as analogous to saying "a dozen eggs" versus "twelve eggs." If you understand what a dozen is, you've reduced twelve single items to one unit!

The Chromatic Scale

Why: You need to understand the ***chromatic scale*** in order to understand just about everything else in music.

What: The chromatic scale includes *all of the notes* (flat, natural, and sharp) *of the musical alphabet*. It starts on any note and goes up (or down) an octave (from A to A, or from C# to C#, for example) in half-steps. Here's the crux of the chromatic scale:

There is a note in between every natural note of the musical alphabet *except between B and C, and E and F*. Each of these "in between" notes can be expressed either as a *sharp* or a *flat.* There is no note—sharp, flat, *or* natural—*between B and C*, or *between E and F*.

Here is an *ascending chromatic scale* from A to A. The notes that are separated by the word "or" are actually the *same note*—with two different names.

A A# or B♭ B C C# or D♭ D D# or E♭ E F F# or G♭ G G# or A♭ A

Here is a *descending chromatic scale* from A to A.

A A♭ or G# G G♭ or F# F E E♭ or D# D D♭ or C# C B B♭ or A# A

2 An *interval* is the distance between two notes.

Different names for the same note are ***enharmonic***—A# and B♭, for example. Think of this as a musical homonym—they sound the same, yet are spelled differently. Calling a note by one or another enharmonic name doesn't change the sound of the note, but there are situations in which it is correct to "spell" the note one way rather than the other. These will be made clear as you read on.

You need to understand the chromatic scale
in order to understand
just about everything else in music.

A more concise way of using ***accidentals*** with the chromatic scale is to split up the enharmonics and use sharps when ascending and flats when descending. Here are chromatic scales from C to C and A to A:

C C# D D# E F F# G G# A A# B **C** B B♭ A A♭ G G♭ F E E♭ D D♭ **C**

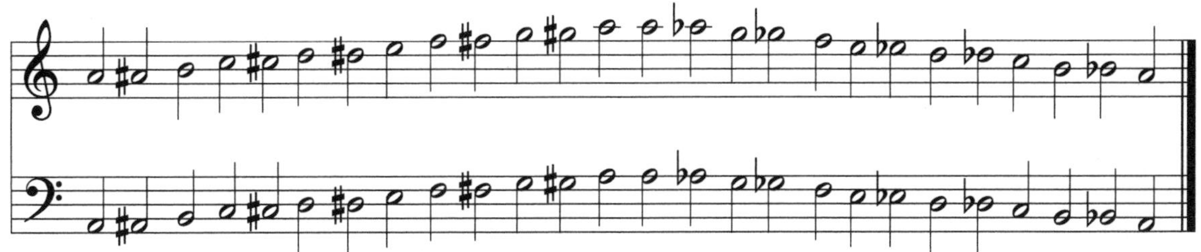

Chromatic Scale from A to A

Before moving on, be clear about the following: every natural note is separated from its next-door natural neighbor by a *whole-step*, *except* the pairs *B and C*, and *E and F*, which are separated by *half-steps*. The chromatic scale is made of only half-steps. There is no note, sharp, flat, or natural, in between B and C, or in between E and F. From B to C is a half-step, and from E to F is a half-step. If you've got all that, then turn the page.

Chapter 2~ The Major Scale

You are now ready to build a major scale upon your solid chromatic foundation. Whether or not you're aware of it, you are surely already *very* familiar with the major scale.

Why: The major scale 𝄞 (good ol' *do re mi fa sol la ti do*) is particularly important in our culture. In fact, much of Western music is based upon it. Try singing it out loud. Chances are good that if you can hold a tune at all, you can sing a major scale. Now try it starting on a lower or higher note. Chances are again good that your ear helped you sing the new major scale correctly. Assuming you *were* able to sing both scales correctly, the reason that they both sounded like major scales was that you maintained the relationships *between the notes* of the scale. Without your consciously being aware of it, your ear followed the formula of what makes a major scale.

Yes indeed, there is a formula.

C Major Scale

If you sing but do not play an instrument, you may not need to know the formula. As soon as you begin playing an instrument, though, or if you want to be a musically literate singer, it becomes helpful to have a specific understanding of the pattern of the scale along with to (perhaps) being able to figure it out by ear. Fasten your seat belt; here comes *the formula*.

What: The major scale has eight notes—seven notes if you take into account that the first and eighth notes are the same note an octave apart. The musical alphabet goes "forward" in an ascending scale, and "backward" in a descending scale, including any sharps and flats needed to make the proper intervals, as follows: the major scale is constructed from *whole-steps*, except *half-steps* between *the third and fourth notes,* and *the seventh and eighth notes*. If you're able to sound out a major scale on your instrument, you'll find that it does indeed follow this pattern.

Use these guidelines to help you choose the correct *enharmonics* as you construct major scales.

1. Never consecutively repeat a letter.

2. Never skip a letter.

Together, these two guidelines mean that every letter (A through G) will be used exactly once, either as a natural, sharp, or flat—except the tonic, which will of course be used twice, at the beginning and end of the scale.

3. Flats and sharps never mix in a major scale. Period. Exclamation point! A major scale can contain either flats *or* sharps, but *not* both.

If that didn't make it easy enough, just remember the half-step between notes 3 and 4. The other half-step (between notes 7 and 8) should take care of itself, because 8 is the same as 1, after all, and a scale must end on the same note with which it began.

For future reference, the "three guiding rules" do not apply to artificial modes, blues, or other scales. They apply only to major scales.

Here are three major scales derived from a chromatic scale. I used my friend Carl's teaching technique of lining up all the notes vertically to make it easier to see the intervals. The tildes (~) are place-holders for the chromatic notes missing from the major scales.

Chromatic Scale (with sharps, then flats):

C	C#	D	D#	E	F	F#	G	G#	A	A#	B	C	C#	D	D#	E
C	D♭	D	E♭	E	F	G♭	G	A♭	A	B♭	B	C	D♭	D	E♭	E
↓	↓	↓	↓	↓	↓	↓	↓	↓	↓	↓	↓	↓	↓	↓	↓	↓

C Major Scale:

1	~	2	~	3	4	~	5	~	6	~	7	8				
C	~	D	~	E	F	~	G	~	A	~	B	C				

D Major Scale:

		1	~	2	~	3	4	~	5	~	6	~	7	8		
		D	~	E	~	F#	G	~	A	~	B	~	C#	D		

E♭ Major Scale:

			1	~	2	~	3	4	~	5	~	6	~	7	8	
			E♭	~	F	~	G	A♭	~	B♭	~	C	~	D	E♭	

If you find this "whole-step place-holder" technique helpful, use a piece of scrap paper (with the chromatic scale at the top, if necessary) to scratch out some major scales. Use your own favorite place-holder. Then fill in the chart on the next page. Count the sharps or flats in each scale and write each scale's total at the far right. Watch out, though: if the tonic of the scale is a flat or sharp note, be sure to count it only *once*, since 1 and 8 are both tonics, and are actually the same note separated by an octave. Right? Right!

The answers to both charts are listed in the answers section, as indicated by the "A" symbol. If "A" is new news, you might want to review the abbreviations on page iv.

Major Scales A

Tonic	2	3	4	5	6	7	(8)	♭s/#s
C	D	E	F	G	A	B	C	0
E								4 #s
B♭								
F								
A								
E♭								
B								
G								
D♭								
A♭								
D								

There is some additional information which I've withheld thus far for the sake of simplicity. It concerns *enharmonics* and *accidentals*. You need this information in order to be able to complete the following four scales correctly. Here goes: Some of the natural notes can *also* be expressed as *sharps* and *flats*, as follows: C = B#, B = C♭, E = F♭, and F = E#. For example, just as an A note, when raised by a half-step, becomes an A#, a B note, when raised by a half-step, becomes a B# (...which is the same as a C...but you already knew that). Keep in mind this new information and the three rules of major scale construction as you complete these scales.

More Major Scales A

Tonic	2	3	4	5	6	7	(8)	♭s/#s
F#								
G♭								
C#								
C♭								

It could be said that there is really only *one major scale*—eight notes separated by whole-steps, except half-steps in between the third and fourth and seventh and eighth notes. The actual notes in this one-and-only major scale are different, though, depending on the tonic. The fifteen major scales you've completed are really different ***transpositions*** of that scale. You'll be introduced to transposition more fully in chapter 18.

Of the major scales you just constructed, three pairs should consist of identical notes, enharmonically re-spelled. These scales are *enharmonic*. Can you find them?

Yes indeed, there is a formula.

Notice also that you can cross-check your scales as you once did (or were supposed to) your math homework. Compare the D and D♭ scales, for instance. Every note in each scale should be a half-step away from the corresponding note in the other scale. Or compare the A and B scales. The corresponding notes should each be a whole-step apart.

Double Sharps and Double Flats

But wait, there's more!! You don't *need* this information immediately, but you will eventually. If you understand what we've done so far, then you're ready for these next tidbits: the double sharp (𝄪) and the double flat (𝄫). It's simple: lower a natural note by two half-steps, and it becomes a double flat. Raise a natural note by two half-steps, and it becomes a double sharp. So, natural notes can also be written as double flats or double sharps.

For example: A → A♭ → A𝄫 (which is the same note as G). Easy! Conversely, raise a note by two half-steps, and it becomes a double sharp. For example: F → F# → F𝄪 (which is the same note as G). Easy again! You won't see double sharps and flats much until you read some more sophisticated music. Until then, off you go.

I'll interrupt our regularly scheduled music theory for this personal note: Have you ever listened to Kurt Weill's second symphony? It's one of my favorite pieces in the world. Also, notice the sublime interaction between the various instruments in the few seconds after the guitar solo on 'Come Together' on the Beatles' *Abbey Road* album. Just wanted you to know.

Write your major scales here.

By the way, the more you practice constructing scales, the faster you'll get at it. With *enough* practice, you'll eventually know scales—or instantly be able to construct them in your head, without ever purposely having memorized them.

The scales in the charts on page 7 were, for the most part, presented in a random order, so you'd concentrate only on each scale's construction. Now you're ready to start to explore scales more deeply, including the scales' *relationships to one another*. In order to do so, though, you need a more flexible and powerful lens to view scales and the notes in them. *Keys* provide that lens.

Chapter 3~ Major Keys and Key Signatures

The major scale construction you've done gives you a *very good linear view* of this important grouping of notes. But its linearity is a bit like being in a tunnel where you can only easily see the note that's directly in front of you. Keys, on the other hand, allow you an *excellent aerial view…* one much better suited to seeing all of the notes at once, as well as the patterns within scales, *and* the relationships *between* different scales. So climb aboard the helicopter and let's go to where you can see the big picture!

What is a *key?* A key is, most simply, the notes of, and chords from, a major scale (or minor scale—but that comes in chapter 11)—*in any order.* 𝄞 For example, a C major scale is in the key of C major. A song that uses the notes of the C major scale is also in the key of C ("in C"). Soon, you will build chords from major scales. These chords are also "in" their respective keys. Finally, songs generally end, and very often begin, on the *tonic* (the first note and chord of the scale). Otherwise, the piece will sound unfinished.

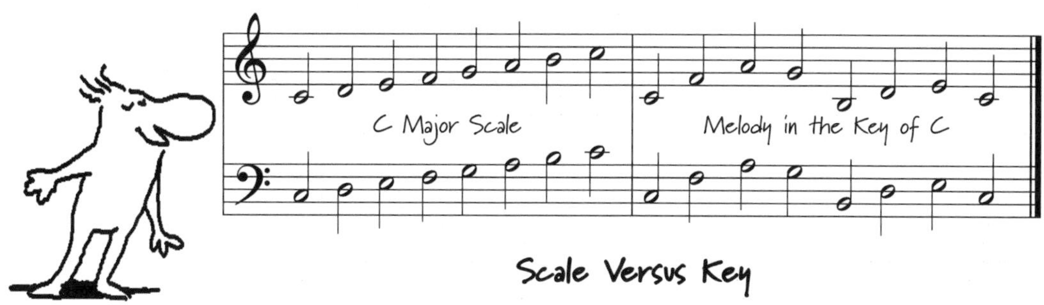

Scale Versus Key

So, a first big difference between a *scale* and its corresponding key is this: in a scale, the notes are in ascending and descending order, whereas in a key, they can be in *any order.* If you scramble 'em all up in any order whatsoever, you still have the notes of that key, but no longer (alas) do you have an intact scale. This is a bit oversimplified, but will hold you over just fine for now.

Why bother learning keys? In addition to the aerial view I mentioned above, there are many benefits similar to those of learning major scales. Instead of keeping track of any number of sharps or flats, you bundle them together into one package—*the key,* and just remember *that*. Finally, most of the music you'll play in your lifetime will be based on the system of keys. Understanding keys will help you understand the music.

Who should bother learning keys? Anyone who plays or sings. That means you.

On this page, you've begun the transition from thinking merely in terms of scale to thinking in terms of key. Let's continue.

"Newest Accidentals"

First off, let's reorder the major scales from least to most accidentals in order to look at *how* flats and sharps are added to them[3]. Go back to the charts on page 7, and using the "number of flats or sharps" columns, fill in the chart below. Rewrite the scales' tonics in the order shown. Then fill in all the sharp or flat notes in each scale. I started it for you.

Major Scales (From Fewest to Most Accidentals) A

Flat Scales/Keys			Sharp Scales/Keys		
How Many Flats?	Tonic	Which Flats?	How Many Sharps?	Tonic	Which Sharps?
1 flat	F	B♭	1 sharp	G	F#
2 flats			2 sharps	D	~~F#~~, C#
3 flats			3 sharps		
4 flats			4 sharps		
5 flats			5 sharps		
6 flats			6 sharps		
7 flats			7 sharps		

Done? Now, look through what you've written and notice this pattern: once a flat shows up for the first time, it appears in all the subsequent flat scales. The same goes for the sharps. For example, F# first appears in the G scale, and continues to appear in every scale with more sharps. See? Pretty nifty, I'd say.

Finally go back and work your way down the scales, crossing out any sharps that have *already appeared* in a previous sharp scale, and any flats that have already appeared in a flat scale. If you do this right, you'll end up with only one accidental left untouched per scale. I crossed out the F# in the D scale for you because it already appeared in the G scale immediately above it. (In fact, all subsequent F#s will also be crossed out for the same reason.)

What you are left with is the "newest sharp or flat" or "newest accidental" added to each scale.

So far, you've learned that flats and sharps are added to major scales in a *systematic* way: all previously added flats or sharps are kept as you go, and there is, therefore, a "newest accidental." Good. Now, let's dig deeper.

3 When scales or keys are viewed in **any** organized order, all kinds of interesting, nifty, important, and **helpful** patterns begin to emerge. Comparing scales with tonics a half-step apart to make sure that **all** of the notes are a half-step apart—as you've done—is an example. You'll see even more after you've learned **The Circle** in chapter 12.

There's another pattern embedded in this "newest accidental" business. It involves the relationship of the newest accidental to its tonic. Using the last chart, figure out *which* ***scale degree***[4] is the newest sharp in *each* of the sharp scales. Which degree is the newest flat (again, in *every* flat scale)? See if you can figure it out before reading further. Really.

The major scale (good ol' "do re mi fa sol la ti do") is particularly important in our culture.

Could you figure it out? The pattern is this: the newest sharp is always the seventh degree of the major scale (and is therefore a *half-step* below the tonic). The newest flat is always the fourth degree of the scale. Always. Reread and remember these. Their importance will be apparent by the end of the chapter, and they'll come in handy for long thereafter.

There are also patterns that allow you to figure out a key in a jiffy. (Pianists: these are especially easy for you because of five-finger positions.) I'll just give you these rather than making you sweat to figure them out.

- *The key with one more sharp (or one fewer flat) starts on the fifth degree of the current key.*

  Let's say that you can't remember which key has one sharp. You *do,* of course, remember that the key of C is all natural. Go to the fifth degree of C: C, D, E, F, G—G is therefore the key with one sharp. What about two sharps? G, A, B, C, D—the key of D has two sharps. Let's say that you know, for some reason, that the key of D♭ has five flats, but you can't remember which key has four. D♭, E♭, F, G♭, A♭—Voilà, it's the key of A♭!

- *The key with one more flat (or one fewer sharp) begins on the fourth degree.*

  For example, let's say you're playing a piece with three flats in the key signature. What key's it in? Watch: C, D, E, F (=1♭); F, G, A, B♭ (=2♭s); B♭, C, D, E♭ (=3♭s). Done.

  Got it? Moving on, I repackaged the previous chart for you on the next page. The sharps and flats are now listed (inside parentheses) in the order *added*, rather than the order they appear in the individual scale. Therefore, the newest flat or sharp will be on the right in each case. Keys are in **bold**. The key of C is included so it won't feel excluded.

---

4 Although "scale degree" sounds very technical, it merely means "note of the scale." So, the first note of the scale (or "tonic") is the first degree, the second note is the second degree, and so on.

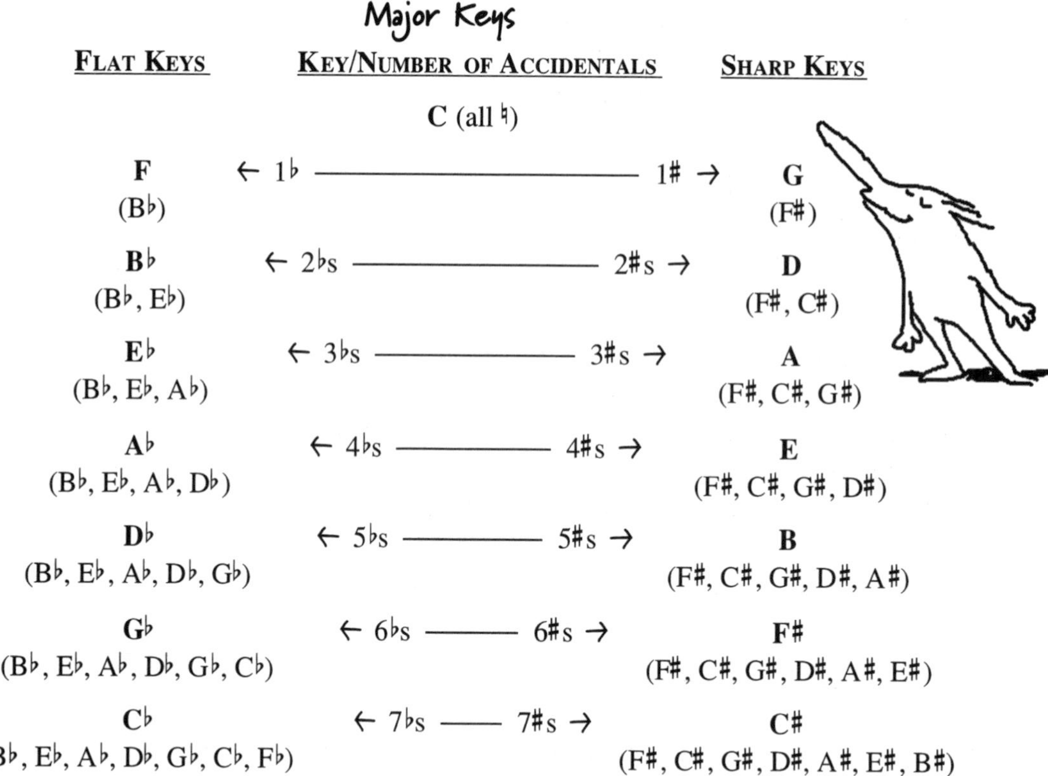

Major Keys

Flat Keys	Key/Number of Accidentals		Sharp Keys
	C (all ♮)		
F (B♭)	← 1♭	1# →	**G** (F#)
B♭ (B♭, E♭)	← 2♭s	2#s →	**D** (F#, C#)
E♭ (B♭, E♭, A♭)	← 3♭s	3#s →	**A** (F#, C#, G#)
A♭ (B♭, E♭, A♭, D♭)	← 4♭s	4#s →	**E** (F#, C#, G#, D#)
D♭ (B♭, E♭, A♭, D♭, G♭)	← 5♭s	5#s →	**B** (F#, C#, G#, D#, A#)
G♭ (B♭, E♭, A♭, D♭, G♭, C♭)	← 6♭s	6#s →	**F#** (F#, C#, G#, D#, A#, E#)
C♭ (B♭, E♭, A♭, D♭, G♭, C♭, F♭)	← 7♭s	7#s →	**C#** (F#, C#, G#, D#, A#, E#, B#)

Key Signatures

Who: This section is mostly for the readers and curious nonreaders among you. All others can skip directly to the next chapter. You folks, do not pass go, and do not collect $200.

What: Once you know how to interpret them, key signatures tell you the key right at the beginning of a piece. Key signatures wrap up all the sharps and flats in a key in one compact package, and display them clearly for all to see. This saves you from the distasteful task of scanning through and figuring out the key sharp by sharp, or flat by flat. Better musicians immediately see, understand, and take note of key signatures. They play much better as a result. Beginners tend not to notice the key signature at all until it's too late… and this comes through all too clearly in their playing.

Key signatures apply to *every occurrence of the included pitches, no matter how high or low, for the entire piece!* [5] Not a bad deal, eh? Set it, and forget it. Again, once you're used to it, this turns out to be *much* more convenient and efficient than scanning through a piece looking for stray accidentals in order to determine the key.

5 Unless a note is modified by a natural (♮) which overrides the flat or sharp in the key signature, but only for any further occurrences of the same note on the same octave, **and** only for the remainder of that measure. This is in contrast to key signatures, which apply to **all** occurrences of the note(s) in question throughout an entire piece, regardless of the octave on which they occur.

Here are the key signatures for the keys of C♯ major and C♭ major. (Again, minor keys will be explained in chapter 11.) These keys, thankfully, have as many sharps and flats as we can possibly have: *all the notes* are either sharp or flat.

Notice that the sharps and flats are *written from left to right in the order added*—an order, which will soon begin to look familiar. So all you need to do to derive any key signature from the ones above is subtract the sharps and flats from the right. For example, if we subtract three flats, we get the key of A♭ major, or F minor, or we can subtract three sharps to get the key of E major or C♯ minor:

This illustrates the advantage of knowing the order in which accidentals are added to keys. The order is always the same; it's just a question of *how many* accidentals you add.

You get the point, right?! So, sharps appear in the following order:

F♯, C♯, G♯, D♯, A♯, E♯, B♯

...and flats appear in the following order:

B♭, E♭, A♭, D♭, G♭, C♭, F♭

Flats and sharps are added in exactly opposite order if you just think of the *letters* and not the *accidentals*. That is, sharps are added from F(♯) to B(♯), and flats are added from B(♭) to F(♭). Cool stuff.

Determining the (Major) Key from a Key Signature

Sharp Keys: To determine the key by looking at a key signature, find the last sharp in the key signature, and go up a half-step. That note will be the tonic. (For example, the key of D has two sharps, F♯ and C♯. The last sharp is the C♯; a half-step higher is D, the tonic of the key.) The reason this technique works is that the "newly added sharp" is always the seventh degree of the scale, and there is a half-step between 7 and 8, right? If that doesn't sound familiar, maybe it's time to review major scale construction.

Flat Keys: In flat keys, the second to the last flat in the key signature *is* the tonic. (For example, the key of B♭ has two flats, B♭ and E♭. The second to the last flat is the B♭—the tonic.) If you use this method, then you just have to *memorize* the key of F, since it only has one flat, and therefore, there *is* no second to the last flat... hmm, perhaps memorization breeds memorization! Read on.

Key Signature Memory Aids

An aside: Honestly, I *hate* memorization! Of course, there are some things that *must* be memorized, but I believe "the less memorization, the better." I'll shut up about it in a second. First, though, I'll echo my friend Tom: "Tools, not rules!" Hear, hear! I think of the system of keys as a *tool* that can help you become a better musician and read and understand music more easily, not as a collection of dead facts to be memorized as quickly as possible. I'd much prefer that you gradually become comfortable with the concepts from this chapter to this point than use the following memory aids. End of speech.

Having said that, here are some admittedly silly phrases which might help you remember the order of added sharps and flats in keys. I couldn't even recite them for you because I don't use them, because I know the notes themselves from having used them over the years. But hey, maybe you're studying for a test next week, and have to commit them to memory fast... just don't get them mixed up until you learn them for real. Even better, *make up your own phrases*. You'll be much more likely to remember them.

By eating Alpo, Doris grew cat fur.

Sharps: F#, C#, G#, D#, A#, E#, B# or, if you'd prefer,

FOR CHOLESTEROL, GREAT DANES ALWAYS EAT BEETS
FAT CATS GIVE DOGS AN ENDLESS BATTLE
FOR CHRISTMAS: GOOSE DOWN AT EVERY BED
FIGHT CANCER: GET DOWN AND EAT BOOGERS
FOREIGN CURRENCY GIVES DOLLARS AN EXTRA BOOST
FRED CAUGHT GAIL DRINKING ALE: EVIL BREW!
FEED COLD GEESE, DUCKS, AND EVEN BEARS
FATHER CARL GOES DOWN AND ENDS BATTLE

Flats: B♭, E♭, A♭, D♭, G♭, C♭, F♭ or, if you'd prefer,

BY EIGHT, ALL DATES GET COLD FEET
BY EATING ANTS, DICK GOT COMPLETELY FAT
BUY ED'S AUTOMATIC DYNAMIC GROWTH COW FEED
BY EATING ALPO, DORIS GREW CAT FUR
BUY EIGHT APPLE DONUTS; GET COFFEE FREE
BATTLE ENDS AND DOWN GOES CARL'S FATHER

There are many other patterns embedded in scales and keys. The more you learn—and *use* what you learn, the more you'll see... and the easier it'll be to remember all of this.

Chapter 4~ Diatonic Intervals

What: Two notes form an ***interval***. An interval is, in general terms, the inclusive distance between two pitches.

Sing a note and then another. This is a *melodic interval*. If two people each sing a different note at the same time, or if you play two notes together on a piano, for example, you instead get a *harmonic interval*. 𝄞

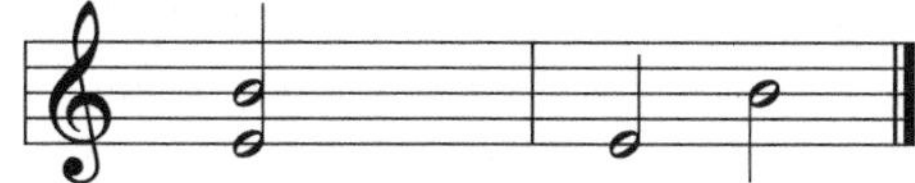

Harmonic and Melodic Perfect Fifth Intervals

The word ***diatonic*** refers to the notes of the major (or minor) scale, as opposed to the chromatic scale. It can also be used generally to mean "drawn directly from a certain scale without chromatic alteration." This chapter introduces you to the diatonic intervals of the major scale.

Why: Learning to recognize intervals, whether by sound, on paper, or on an instrument, is extremely helpful for many reasons. Among them are chord building, improvisation, ***sight-singing***, composition, understanding and remembering keys and their related accidentals, and figuring out music by ear. If you are trying to play a melody that is in your head or on the radio, knowing your intervals eliminates most of the time spent searching for the right notes.

How: Intervals can be named *generally* by merely counting upwards (by going forwards using the letters of the musical alphabet) from one note to the other, inclusively. For example, from C to E is a third (C to C is 1, or more commonly and elegantly, a *unison*, C to D is a second and finally, C to E is a third.) Count on your fingers if it helps; I won't tell. "C, D, E; 1, 2, 3!"

Unfortunately, this tells only part of the story. For example, C to E♭ is also a third, as are E to G and E to G#. If you count the half-steps in these thirds—using the chromatic scale, of course—you'll immediately see that they are of two different sizes. Sure enough, the intervals C to E♭ and E to G are both made of three half-steps, whereas C to E and D to F# are *four* half-steps! But these three intervals are, by definition all thirds! Obviously, we need a more specific way to categorize intervals. Don't touch that dial, viewers at home…

What we have avoided thus far is defining the *type* or *quality* of the interval. Let's stop avoiding it! To measure and define intervals accurately, we need both the *size* (a number) *and* the *type* of interval (for example, *major third*, or *perfect fifth*). Types of intervals include *perfect (P), major (M), minor (m), diminished (°),* and *augmented (+).* Learning the correct names, or the *quality* of intervals may at first seem to be a nit-picky affair. The fact is, it's not *that* hard, and *does* help in understanding chords, not to mention communicating with other musicians. Whoops, I mentioned it.

Here's a chart of the intervals that occur in the major scale. 𝄞 For each interval, the following information is given: the correct interval name including number and quality; the number of half-steps between the two notes, and an example of the interval built on C.

Diatonic Intervals from an Octave to a Unison

INTERVAL	HALF-STEPS	C EXAMPLE
P Octave	12	C - C
M7	11	C - B
M6	9	C - A
P5	7	C - G
P4	5	C - F
M3	4	C - E
M2	2	C - D
P Unison	0	C - C

Diatonic Intervals from a Unison to an Octave

Notice that the intervals which occur from the tonic of a major scale up to any note in the scale are either *perfect* or *major*. In other words, there are no minor, diminished, or augmented intervals built upward from the tonic of a major scale.

Go back to the chapter on keys, and use your newfound knowledge of intervals to answer these questions: What is the interval between each added sharp? (Regardless of their printed octave, use only ascending intervals for now, i.e., F# *up* to C#.) Each added flat? By what interval does the tonic move as you add sharps? As you add flats? A

Now that you've been introduced to the major scale and the diatonic intervals, the groundwork has been laid for you to understand chords. Don't look now; here they come!

Chapter 5~ Chords: Triads

What is a chord? Ah, the good questions just keep a-comin'! A chord is a collection of *three or more* notes in a specific pattern of stacked intervals—usually thirds. In twentieth century harmony, chords are also built of fourths, as well as other intervals—yup, almost anything goes these days! We will mostly stick to chords built in thirds, and begin with the simplest and smallest chords: ***triads***. A triad is a three note chord.

How do chords differ from scales? They differ in several ways. First, the intervals which make up scales are mostly seconds, although some thirds creep in, depending on the scale. Chords, on the other hand, are mostly made of thirds, as I said. Second, if you were to play an entire scale all at once on a piano, for instance, the sound would be very dense, to say the least. Chords, on the other hand, are very commonly played all at once, although they can be, and are, certainly also played one note at a time. (This is called *arpeggiating* a chord. *Arpeggio* is from the Italian *arpeggiare*—to play the harp. An arpeggio is a *broken chord*, or a chord played one note at a time.) Lastly, and very importantly, *chords are derived from scales*, although it's also possible to build chords by *stacking intervals*.

Overview of Basic Chord Anatomy

Chord names can be separated into two parts: the *chord root,* and the *chord suffix*. The *root* tells you what note the chord is built upon. Any note of the chromatic scale (natural, flat, or sharp) can be the root of a chord. The *suffix* tells you the chord *quality* or *type*. There are many types of chords. They include major, minor, seventh, major ninth, minor eleventh flat five, and many more. If a chord has no suffix, it is understood to be a major triad. That is, a chord is understood to be major unless something else is specified.

How: If you take the first, third, and fifth note of a major scale and stack them up, you get a major triad. Specifically, you get the major triad built on the first note of that scale. 𝄞

C major scale: **C** D **E** F **G** A B C
1 2 **3** 4 **5** 6 7 8

C major chord: C E G
1 3 5

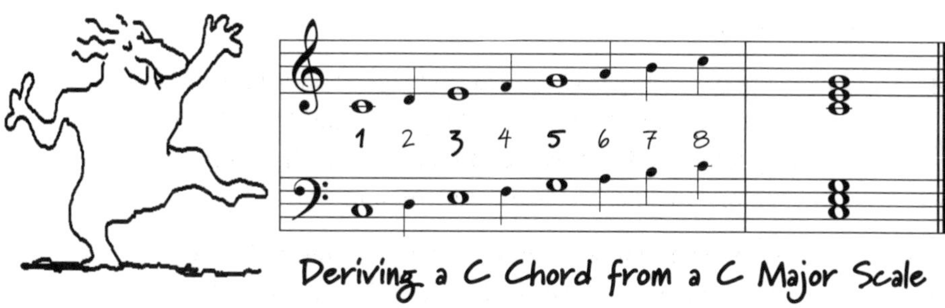

Deriving a C Chord from a C Major Scale

Let's make it into a formula: a major chord (triad) = 1, 3, 5. This definition applies not only to a C chord, but to *any* major triad.

We can also define a major chord by counting the half steps between the notes: C to E is four half-steps, and E to G is three half-steps. Please don't take my word for it; count them yourself! So, a major chord can be defined as having four half steps from the root to the third, and three half-steps from the third to the fifth. While this is certainly true, the first method is more efficient assuming you know your scales… which you do, right?

Creating Minor Intervals

Another way of defining a major chord requires you to know how to construct minor intervals. Here's how you make a major interval minor. If you lower the top note of a major interval by a half-step, it becomes a minor interval. For example: C to E is a major third, so C to E♭ is a minor third. D to F# is a major third, so D to F is a minor third. C to A and E to C# are major sixths, so C to A♭ and E to C are minor sixths. It's easy.

You can now define the major triad in terms of your newly learned intervals: a major third from the root to the third, and a minor third from the third to the fifth.

Let's pull out all the stops[6] and define the rest of the triads. The following chart includes the patterns of stacked major and minor thirds which make up each triad. (The suspended chord is an exception to the "stacked thirds" rule, consisting of a stacked perfect fourth and major second.) 𝄞

When using numbers to define a chord or scale, a flat preceding a scale degree means "lowered," and a sharp means "raised." For example, ♭3 is a chromatically lowered third, and #5 is a raised fifth. The resulting lowered or raised note itself may be flat, natural, or sharp, depending on what the original note was.

Triads 𝄞

Name (Chord Type)	Abbreviation	Spelling			Stacked Thirds	C Sample 𝄞		
major	✣ none, or Δ	1	3	5	major, minor	C	E	G
minor	m, –	1	♭3	5	minor, major	C	E♭	G
diminished	°, dim	1	♭3	♭5	minor, minor	C	E♭	G♭
augmented	+, aug	1	3	#5	major, major	C	E	G#
suspended	4, sus, sus 4	1	4	5	P4, M2	C	F	G

✣ A chord is a major triad unless specified otherwise.

Examples: E♭ = E♭ major   A = A major   F#m = F# minor   G♭– = G♭ minor

6 This fine expression comes from the world of church organs, of all things. The stops of an organ control the flow of air to the pipes. Pulling out all the stops makes all the organ's pipes active, ensuring a big, big sound, and increased pulse rate in all those listening.

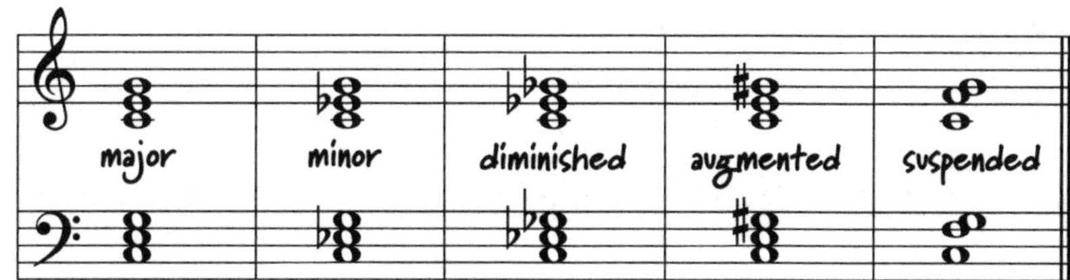

Triads Built On C

Try associating the meaning of the names of the diminished, augmented, and suspended chords with the construction of each chord. *Diminish* means *to make smaller*, and indeed, everything except the root of this chord is lowered. *Augment* means *to increase*. In the augmented chord, the fifth is raised. Finally, the sound of the suspended chord leaves you hanging. It 'wants' to resolve to the major or minor triad built on the same root.

While all of the chord building methods I've talked about are usable, the '1, 3, 5 method' turns out to be the most universally helpful. There are many, many, different types of chords, and as soon as one begins working with chords more complex than triads, the other methods fall short. So, from this chapter, take this with you: a major chord is 1, 3, and 5, from its major scale. Are we in accord?

Ear-Training Preview

By playing these different chords on an instrument, you can begin to associate each chord with its sound. Chords have both *absolute sounds* and *subjective associations. Absolute sound* is difficult to describe, and has to be learned as you become familiar with each chord. (This is analogous to describing colors in absolute terms. Imagine describing a color to someone who was born blind.)

Subjective associations are easier to put into words. Major and minor chords sound *stable* or *resolved.* They could be used to end a song. Diminished and augmented chords are *unstable.* If they were used at the end of a song, it would sound decidedly unfinished. Instead, they are used as *passing chords*— they *pull* one stable chord to another. More specifically, most of us hear major chords as *happy, heroic,* or *strong*, minor chords as *sad, lonesome,* or *haunting*, diminished chords as *suspenseful* and *haunting*, and augmented chords as *dreamy, strange,* and *eerie.*

On a completely unrelated topic, remember to listen to William Walton's First Symphony frequently. Sometimes, I forget for a while and then remember. Then I'm glad I remembered. My favorite recording is *the Scottish National Orchestra* with Alexander Gibson pitching, on the Chandos label.

What's yours?

Chapter 6—
Diatonic Harmony

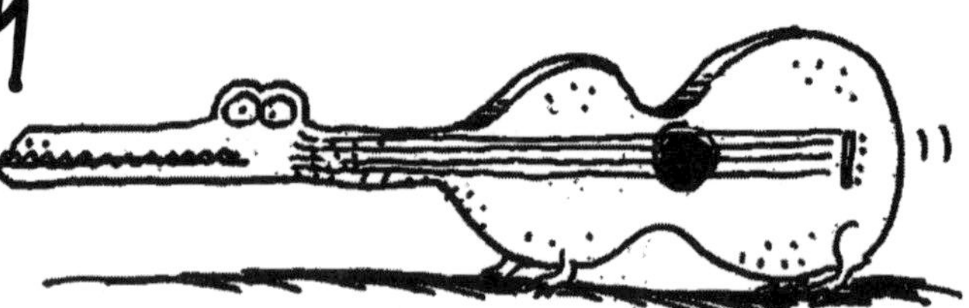

Harmonizing a Major Scale

What happens if you harmonize a major scale with itself? You get something important and relevant to musicians: diatonic[7] harmony. Anything occurring in the major scale—that is, without changing any notes, or adding any notes from outside the scale—is *diatonic*. This could include diatonic notes, intervals, chords, melodies, etc.

Why might you care? Because a harmonized major scale is almost as common as the major scale itself. You've heard it everywhere in various guises, from Bach to Mariachi to Greek music to Crosby, Stills, & Nash. *It just won't go away!*

How do you go about harmonizing a scale? Grab a friend (gently). Sing a major scale with one of you beginning two notes after the other. Or start at the same time; one of you on the first note of the scale, the other on the third. 𝄞 Either of these will give you a major scale harmonized in diatonic thirds. Or, sing (or play on an instrument of your choice) the bottom voice up an octave, or the top voice down an octave, and you'll get the scale in diatonic sixths, as notated below. 𝄞

Let's talk for a moment about diatonic thirds and sixths. In the key of C, diatonic thirds are C (up) to E, D to F, E to G, and so on. 𝄞 Of these, notice that C to E is a major third, but D to F and E to G are minor thirds. Diatonic sixths are C (up) to A, D to B, E to C, F to D, and so on. Notice again that the diatonic sixths are both major and minor. So it goes with diatonic intervals. Diatonic intervals are different sizes, or *qualities*, depending on what degree of the scale they're built upon. As long as there are no notes added from outside the key, the harmony is still diatonic… and diatonic harmony is, after all, the name of this chapter.

Theoretically, any interval *could* be used for this, but some sound "better" than others. Thirds and sixths have been the intervals of choice for hundreds of years. Various types of rock have reclaimed fourths and fifths for their comparatively hollow sound. Harmonizing in seconds and sevenths results in a markedly dissonant sound. This technique is often used by arrangers and composers for effects ranging from macabre to comical. Give these all a try!

7 **Diatonic** (as opposed to **chromatic**) means using the notes of a major (or minor) scale, without changing or adding any notes by adding or subtracting flats or sharps. This is **not** the same thing as **Diet Tonic**, either.

For our purposes now, let's agree on the cultural favorite of harmonizing the major scale in diatonic thirds or sixths. Fill in the *qualities*—major (M) or minor (m)—of the resulting intervals.

C Major Scale Harmonized in Diatonic Thirds & Sixths

- Calling all you bass clef readers: as I mentioned in the Prelude, many (or most) of the bass clef notation examples need to be played an octave (or more) higher in order not to sound muddy. I just didn't want to leave you folks out or use tons of ledger lines.
- In the following charts, the scale degrees continue beyond the octave. Don't worry. You will use these "beyond the octave" intervals extensively later for building "higher extensions": ninth, eleventh, and thirteenth chords.

Major Scale: Diatonic Harmonization In Thirds 𝄞

Top Instrument/Voice:	3	4	5	6	7	8	9	(10)
Bottom Instrument/Voice:	1	2	3	4	5	6	7	(8)
Resulting Intervals:	M	___	___	___	___	___	___	(___)

Or, in the key of C: 𝄞

Top Instrument/Voice:	E	F	G	A	B	C	D	(E)
Bottom Instrument/Voice:	C	D	E	F	G	A	B	(C)

Major Scale: Diatonic Harmonization In Sixths 𝄞

Top Instrument/Voice:	1	2	3	4	5	6	7	(8)
Bottom Instrument/Voice:	3	4	5	6	7	8	9	(10)
Resulting Intervals:	m	___	___	___	___	___	___	(___)

Or, in the key of C: 𝄞

Top Instrument/Voice:	C	D	E	F	G	A	B	(C)
Bottom Instrument/Voice:	E	F	G	A	B	C	D	(E)

Diatonic Triads

What: If you add another diatonic third on top of the diatonic thirds you've just made, you'll get *diatonic triads*—chords consisting only of notes from the major scale; one chord built on each note of the scale. You already completed the first step of this process when you constructed a major triad built on the ***tonic***[8].

Why would we want diatonic chords? I'll tell you, but no more questions so close to bed-time. It's because the chords which arise from harmonizing the major scale are just as important and common as the scale itself—*very, very common.* In fact, diatonic chords are the first place to look when figuring out the chords to a song, or when trying to make sense of a chord progression. The simpler the song or piece, the more likely that the chords will be diatonic. Also, understanding diatonic chords is the first step towards understanding more complicated chord progressions.

How does a regular ol' person go about harmonizing the major scale in order to come up with these legendary diatonic chords? Ok, *one last* answer 'til tomorrow. Again, one simply stacks two *diatonic thirds* upon each note of the major scale. Another way to think of this is merely skipping notes in the scale: 1, 3, 5 for the first chord (that should look familiar); 2, 4, 6 for the second chord; 3, 5, 7 for the third, and so on.

Before we build the diatonic chords in the key of C, let me mention that this all is much easier to see in music notation than in words and numbers. Are you still a music notation hold-out? This alone would be a good reason to get going with it, but, enough preaching.

In the following notation example is a C major scale harmonized in thirds. This gives us the *diatonic triads* in the key of C. 𝄞 After some help on the next page or so, come back and fill in the name of each chord.

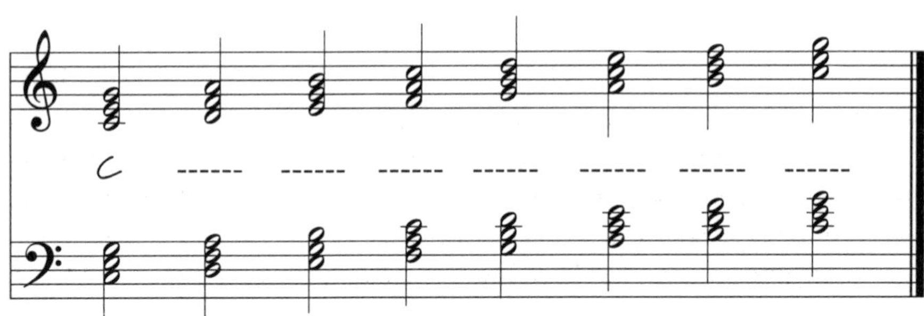

Diatonic Triads in the Key of C

8 Again, the **tonic** is the first note of a scale... or the chord built on the first note of a scale.

The following chart—for the nonreaders—is essentially three horizontal C major scales, each offset by a third from the one below. In other words, the bottom one begins on C, the tonic of the C major scale, the middle one begins on E, a third higher, and the top one begins yet another third higher on the fifth of the scale: G. These *horizontal scales* give us vertical *diatonic triads*.

Diatonic Triads in C

Name	Tonic	Supertonic	Mediant	Subdominant	Dominant	Submediant	Leading Tone
Scale Degree	**1**	**2**	**3**	**4**	**5**	**6**	**7**
Fifth	G	A	B	C	D	E	F
Third	E	F	G	A	B	C	D
Root	C	D	E	F	G	A	B
Chord Name	C						

Meet the diatonic degrees by name in the top row. The ones you should *absolutely* get to know by name are the tonic, subdominant, and dominant. They come up a lot. The other names (supertonic, mediant, submediant, and leading tone) are very rarely heard in everyday use—you needn't bother with them unless you want to; they *do* come in handy at cocktail parties and music theory exams, though.

In the chart, the eighth scale degree is omitted since it's the same as the tonic.

The **Root**, **Third,** and **Fifth** headings at the left of the chart apply to *each chord.* In other words, the *Tonic* column shows the root, third, and fifth of the chord built on the first note of the scale—the tonic; the *Supertonic* column shows the root, third, and fifth of the chord built on the second note of the scale—the supertonic, and so on.

Now, to determine the *type* for each chord, compare each triad with the major triad built on the same root, and see how it differs. For example, the chord built on the second degree of the C scale is D, F, and A. Compare that to a D major triad by constructing a D major scale, and extracting one, three, and five to get a D major triad: D, F#, and A. 𝄞 You can see that the root and fifth of the chord are the same, but the third has been changed. Specifically, the third has been lowered a half-step. This means that the diatonic chord built on the second degree of the C major scale is a D minor.

Comparing Dm to D

Continue with this process to define the five remaining diatonic chords. They should all be either major, minor, or diminished. If any of them doesn't fit one of these definitions, you've made a mistake somewhere. Then fill in the following information. A

What are the diatonic chords in the key of C? C Dm ____ ____ ____ ____ ____

Major chords are built on which degrees of the major scale? ____ ____ ____

Minor chords are built on which degrees? ____ ____ ____

A diminished chord is built on which degree? ____

The beauty of learning the pattern of diatonic chords is similar to the beauty of learning the major scale pattern: one size fits all... or, one pattern fits all keys. In other words, the pattern you derived above applies to *all* keys, not just the key of C. To get the pattern of diatonic triads in all keys, leave out the root names, and write only the chord *type*. A

major minor ______ ______ ______ ______ ______

But that's a package which is hard to hold. So, common practice is to use Roman numerals to show the scale degrees upon which chords are built; upper case (capital letters) for any chords containing major thirds, and lower case (small letters) for all chords containing minor thirds. Depending on who is doing the writing, minor chords sometimes are written with an "m" after the Roman numeral just to make absolutely sure you've gotten the point (as in this book, for example). Diminished chords get their customary "o" abbreviation.

Now, rewrite the pattern of diatonic triads for all keys: A

I iim ____ ____ ____ ____ ____

There, that's better. I hope these points struck a chord in you. Diatonic chords will come up again in this book. More important, they are everywhere in the music you listen to and play. Now that you are aware of them, you'll have a satisfying "uh-huh" experience every time you happen upon them. You are also on your way to understanding more complex chord progressions. Onward.

Chapter 7~ Chord Inversion

What: So far, we've been dealing with chords in ***root position***. Root position simply means that the root is the lowest note in the chord—the remaining notes are stacked on top. But, you can also change the order of the notes, thereby *inverting* a chord.

How: You can invert a chord simply by transposing (moving) the lowest note of the chord up an octave, while leaving the others untouched. You can also invert *downwards* by transposing the *highest* note of the chord *down* an octave.

If you take a root position chord, and transpose the lowest note (the root) up an octave, the chord is now in *first inversion.* Now put the new lowest note (the third) up an octave, and you get a *second inversion* chord. If you now transpose the fifth up an octave, the chord will be back in root position, only an octave higher. A triad must always be in one of these three inversions. Here is a chart showing the inversion of a C major chord—C, E, and G—as well as any major chord—1, 3, and 5. Notice that the circled notes with dark arrows move up an octave (and become **bold**) in each case.

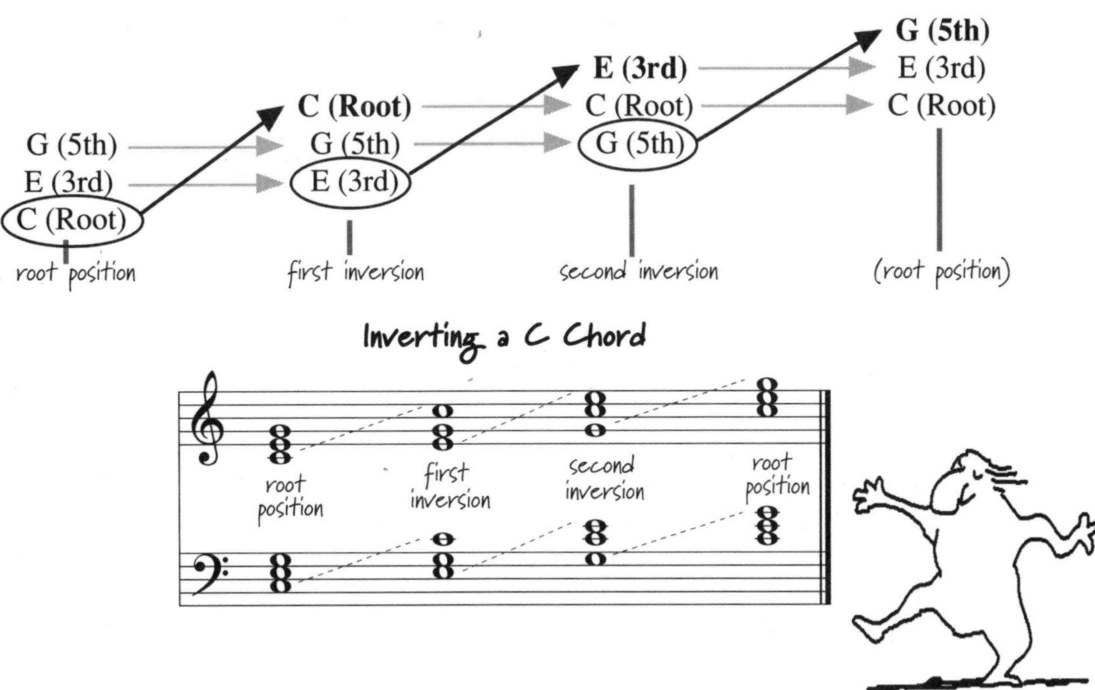

Chords can theoretically have as many inversions as they have notes.
I say "theoretically" because larger chords tend to be more fussy about their inversions; some inversions definitely sound better than others. Triads and seventh chords (soon to be introduced) can, for most practical purposes, be freely inverted, depending on context.

Why invert? I thought you'd never ask. There are many reasons. In common practice, chord progressions are *not* generally successions of root position chords moving one to the other (except in heavy metal music, in which whole songs of only root position chords are commonly the case). In most other types of music, progressions are made up of *individual* ***chord-tones***[9] moving independently from *notes in one chord* to *notes in the next chord*, creating melodic lines, which are often called *voices*, because the resulting melodies could be sung or played by individual instruments. So, chord *progressions* (any series of chords) sound better with root position chords mixed with inverted chords, so various notes of one chord lead smoothly to notes in the next chord, with others perhaps not moving at all. This is called *voice-leading*. (A thorough introduction to voice-leading is beyond the scope of this book. Refer to any good counterpoint book or course.)

Another reason for inversion, especially important for string instruments, is to make the chord easier (or in many cases, possible) to reach. Many chords—especially ones with four or more notes—are virtually unplayable in root position on instruments such as guitar and mandolin.

Here are three examples of a C, Am, F, G, C chord progression. 𝄞 In the nonreaders' chart below, the notes that make up the chords are written vertically above the chord names, which are in **bold**. The chord-tones are written so that all occurrences of the same note occur on the same line. Try playing these on your instrument.

In the first example, the chords are all in root position. Notice how the chords jump from one to the other. It's as if the chords *coexist*, but don't particularly *interact*. In moving from C to Am, for example, the G note must jump down a minor third to the E note, or each whole chord must move by a third… not exactly smooth voice-leading! Next come two versions of the same progression with the chords inverted to make the voice-leading as smooth as possible. Notice that only the G note moves (to A) between the C to Am chords. Moving from the Am to the F chord, only the E note moves to an F. The other notes of the chords stay in place. This use of ***common tones*** (notes shared by two chords in succession) makes the voice-leading smooth.

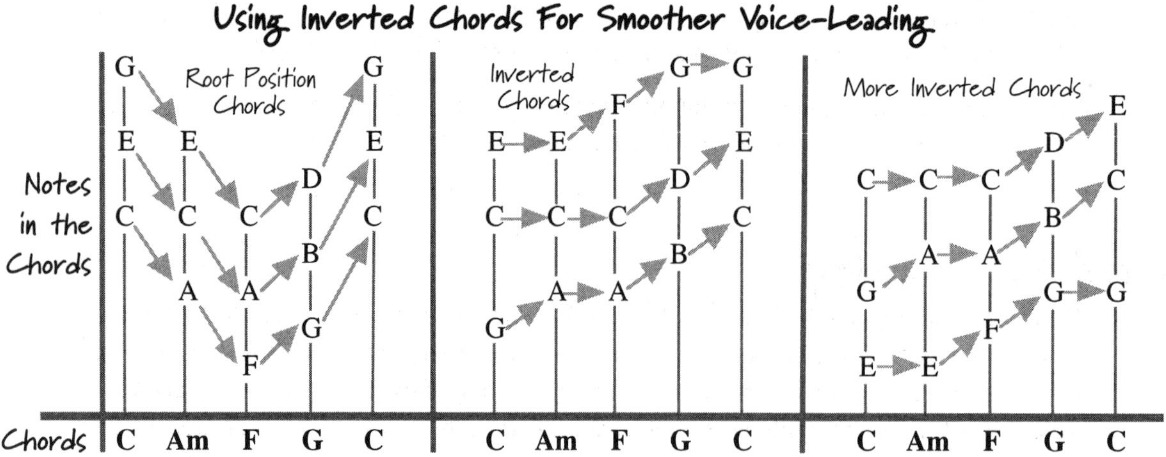

9 A **chord-tone** is simply any note in a chord.

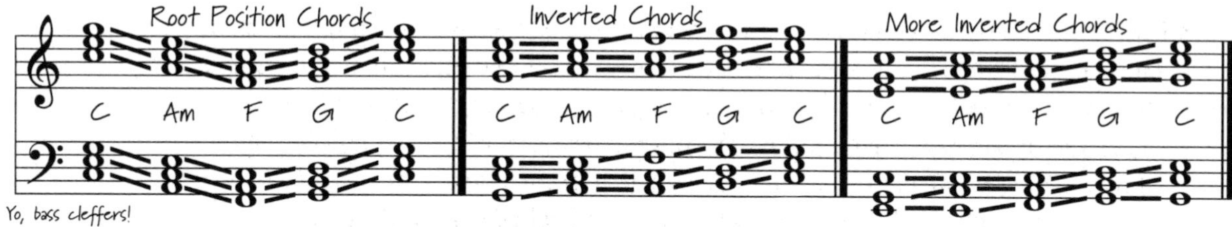

Chord Progression in Root Position and Inverted

Determining the Root and Chord Type of an Unknown Chord

If you run across a chord that you are unable to identify, invert the chord until you get a chord made of stacked thirds. The root will then be the lowest note. Then use your—soon to be extensive—knowledge of chord structure to determine the chord type. 𝄞

Identifying a Chord by Inverting It to Root Position

The notation example turns out to be a B major chord, after a bit of inverting. After you've worked with chords for a while, you'll instantly be able to identify chords in *any* inversion. Trust me.

Chords containing intervals other than thirds are trickier. These include suspended triads (and sixth and minor sixth chords, to be introduced in chapter 13). Fear not, though, you will soon be comfortable enough with these to be able to identify them easily.

Again, bass cleffers: play your notation examples an octave higher where necessary. Otherwise, they'll sound muddy: wash your ears or people will point and smirk.

Chord-Tone Doubling

We've been talking about chords as if they were always voiced with only one occurrence of each note in the chord. In real life, chord-tones are often *doubled* (duplicated) on more than one octave. If you have the luxury of having enough fingers and/or strings and/or players to allow you to double notes in a chord, here is the textbook order of most to least preferable: root, fifth, third, then everything else. This is also context, style, and voice-leading dependent. In many cases, you will double the melody note and the bass note.

Chapter 8~ Chromatic Intervals

Why: Diatonic intervals are okay, but they are only part of the story. Intervals of various sizes are often equally important. It's time to break out of the safety of diatonic intervals.

What: Intervals including those *not* found in the major scale. The following chart and notation example show the chromatic intervals from an octave down to a unison, along with their size in half-steps, and an example built on C. 𝄞 Those intervals that occur in the major scale are pointed out (☞).

Chromatic Intervals from Octave to Unison

	INTERVAL	SIZE IN HALF-STEPS	C EXAMPLE
☞	P Octave	12	C - C
☞	M7	11	C - B
	m7 (+6)	10	C - B♭ (A♯)
☞	M6	9	C - A
	m6 (+5)	8	C - A♭ (G♯)
☞	P5	7	C - G
	°5 or +4	6	C - G♭ or C - F♯
☞	P4	5	C - F
☞	M3	4	C - E
	m3 (+2)	3	C - E♭ (D♯)
☞	M2	2	C - D
	m2 (+U)	1	C - D♭ (C♯)
☞	P Unison	0	C - C

Chromatic Intervals From Unison to an Octave (Common Enharmonics)

Chromatic Alteration of Intervals

So far, we've looked at intervals as individuals. Now, let's see some of the ways in which they relate to each other in polite society and parties. Knowing the following rules will help you especially in forming and altering chords. Refer to the **Chromatic Intervals from Octave to Unison** chart, and notice that the following statements are indeed true.

1. When the top (higher) note of a *major* interval is lowered, the interval becomes a *minor* interval.
2. When the top note of a *minor* interval is lowered, the interval becomes a *diminished* interval.
3. When the top note of a *perfect* interval is lowered, the interval becomes a *diminished* interval.
4. When the top note of a *perfect* interval is raised, the interval becomes an *augmented* interval.
5. When the top note of a *major* interval is raised, the interval becomes an *augmented* interval.

Less Common Enharmonic Spellings of Intervals

This section is included here for the sake of completeness. If you've just *loved* intervals so far, you may well also love this. If you just skimmed over intervals, this won't mean much to you, so skip onward. You can always come back. Relax.

Still with me? Great; here goes: Rather than list every theoretical possibility, I'll limit myself to those examples which most people are likely to come across *in this lifetime.* You can read more books next lifetime, and there's still plenty of time in this lifetime for books more fussy than this one.

m7 = +6 ....C - A# (found especially in Romantic era classical music)

M6 = °7................................C - B𝄫 (found in diminished seventh chords)

m6 = +5................................C - G# (found in augmented triads)

m3 = +2................................C - D#

m2 = + Unison.....................C - C#

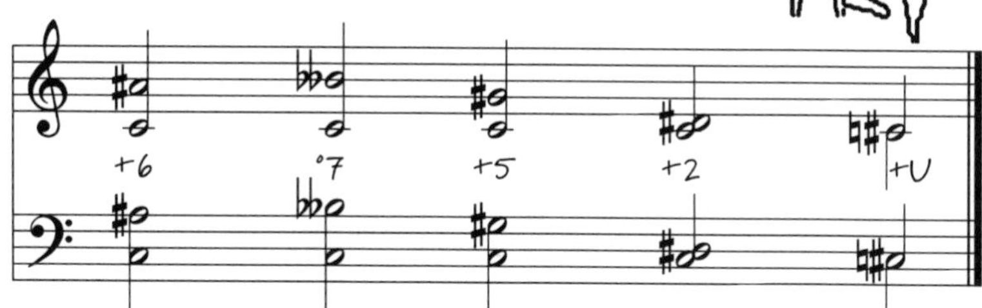

Some Less Common Enharmonic Spellings of Intervals

Chapter 9~
I, IV, V and the Twelve Bar Blues

What: When you wrote out the diatonic chords you discovered that three of them were major. They are those built on the first, fourth, and fifth degrees of the scale. These (notes and chords) are the *tonic*, *subdominant*, and *dominant*, respectively. The relationship between *tonic* and *dominant* is the strongest and most important relationship in Western music. The *subdominant* chord comes next in line.

Why: A lot of Baroque, Classical, and Romantic period classical music can be reduced to these three chords. Quite a bit of African pop, Calypso, Reggae, '50s, and '60s rock 'n' roll, many different types of folk music, and children's songs, are often *nothing but these chords*. That covers *a lot!* Chew on this, then swallow: the simpler the song, the more likely it is that the chords will boil down to just *I*, *V*, and *IV*, in that order of frequency. *The Farmer in the Dell,* for example, is made up of just *I* and *V*. 𝄞

I **I**
The farmer in the dell, the farmer in the dell
I **I V I**
hi-ho the derry-o, the farmer in the dell.

I I I I V I

Gee, I'd play this bass clef example up an octave if I were me...

The Farmer in the Dell: Tonic & Dominant Harmony

If you were on a particularly tight harmonic budget, you *could* get away with accompanying the *Farmer in the Dell* merely with the I chord. Personally, I'd miss that one *V* chord, though.

Old MacDonald, on the other hand, pretty much *needs* the *I* and *V* chords, and definitely sounds much richer with the inclusion of a *IV* chord. 𝄞

I **IV I I V I**
Old MacDonald had a farm, ee-i, ee-i-oh.

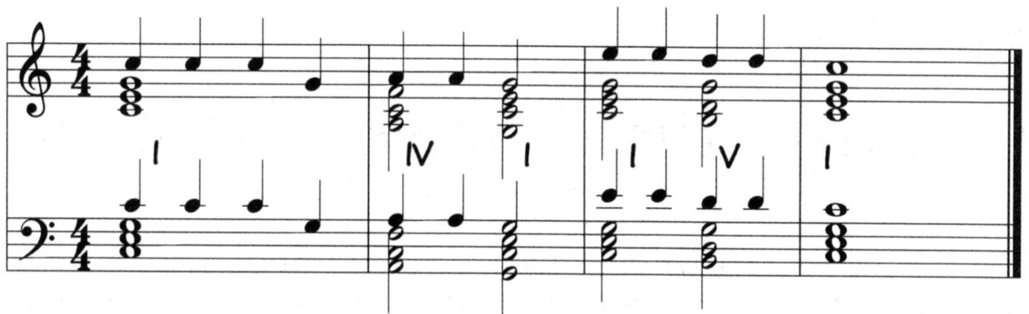

Old MacDonald: Tonic, Subdominant, & Dominant Harmony

Many folk songs such as *Oh Susannah* can be played with just these three chords, although some additional chords certainly dress it up. We'll dress Susannah in fancier threads in upcoming chapters. 𝄞

IV   **I**   **V**   **I**   **I**   **V**   **I**
Oh, Susannah, don't you cry for me, for I come from Alabama with my banjo on my knee.

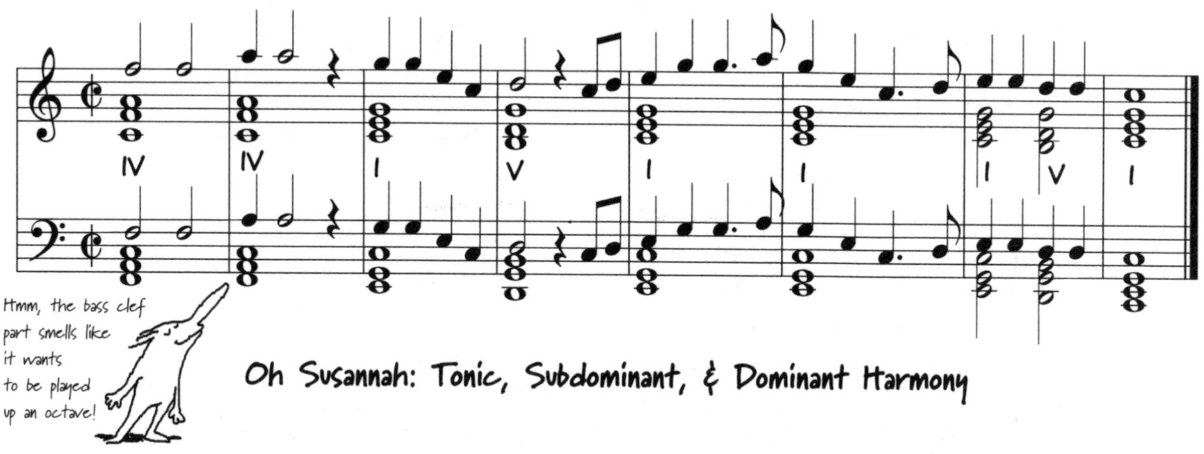

Oh Susannah: Tonic, Subdominant, & Dominant Harmony

Okay, now try playing these chord progressions on the instrument of your choice. Play each chord for a measure (four beats), as written, in the style and rhythm of your choice.

‖: **I** | **IV** | **I** | **V** :‖

‖: **I** | **IV** | **V** | **IV** :‖

‖: **I** | **I** | **IV** | **V** :‖

These (|) are bar lines. They show you the beginning and end of measures. The double lines with double dots (‖: :‖) are repeat signs. Repeat whatever is inside them.

These are three common "one-four-five" progressions. There are many. One of the most important "one-four-five" progressions is the *twelve bar blues*.

Twelve Bar Blues~ Part I

Why? The twelve bar blues is one of the most important song forms in folk, jazz, rock, and popular music. Understand the twelve bar blues and its variations, and you will understand hundreds or thousands of songs. Not a bad investment of energy; wouldn't you say? We'll start by analyzing the structure of the lyrics, and then move to the harmony.

Blues Phrase Structure

The roots of the blues can be traced back to traditional African music. One aspect of this inheritance is the use of call and response. The twelve bar blues, the most common blues form, consists of *three lines of four bars each*. Each line consists of an approximately two bar statement often followed by an (implicit or explicit) response. If the particular blues song is being sung (as opposed to being played on an instrument), the response can be sung by the rest of the band, or played on an instrument, or even several instruments. Sometimes, the response is only hinted at; sometimes it is omitted entirely.

Play, sing, or think of these examples "in four" at first, that is, four beats to a measure, since a lot of blues tends to be in four. Here's a skeletal example of twelve bar blues showing a typical statement and response pattern (again, the vertical lines are bar lines):

state-	ment	response	
restate-	ment	response	
whatcha	gonna do?	(response)	

Here's an example of a generic blues lyric. Notice how well this one fits the pattern.

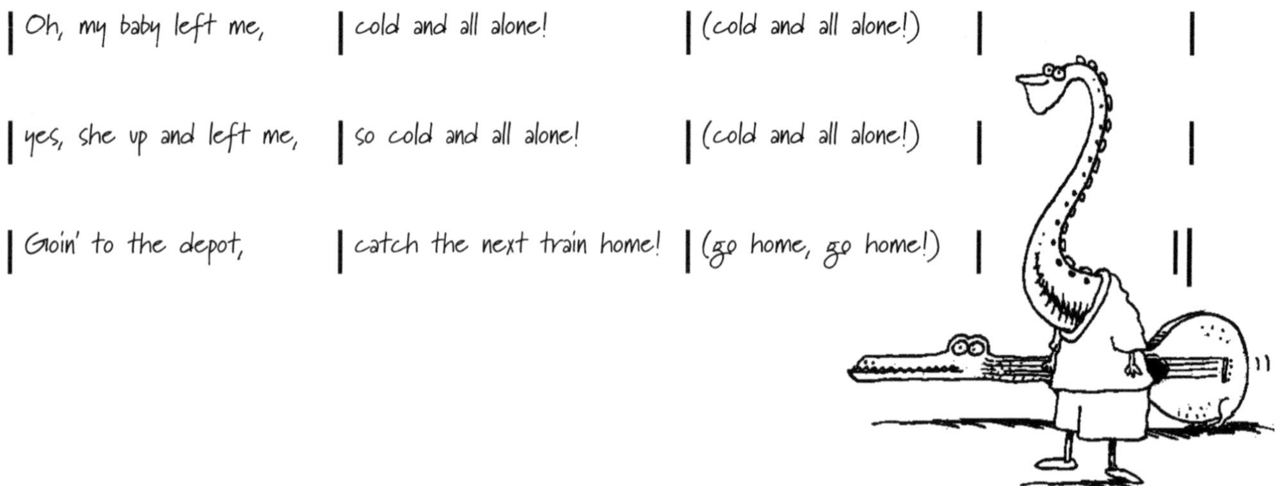

Blues Chordology

The *I*, *IV*, and *V* chords form the backbone of the blues, and any music based on the blues. These first two twelve bar blues progressions are as simple as they are common. Many of the fine, renowned blues players never get much more harmonically complex than this. On the other hand, many very complex jazz blues are based on these same progressions. In both of these, and in most blues-based contexts, you can make the major chords into *dominant sevenths*[10] (1, 3, 5, ♭7), or even *ninths*[10] (1, 3, 5, ♭7, 9), pretty much at will (use your ears, and try to get to the point where you know what is, and is not, commonly done in the musical styles of your choice).

The slashes (/) in the following progressions represent the beats of the measure. These chord slashes take any potential guesswork out of figuring out how many beats a chord lasts. They are standard in jazz notation. They are place-holders, and don't dictate a specific rhythm; rhythmic notation is used to show specific rhythms.

1. bare-bones, no-frills, no-padding-on-the-seats, pay-for-refills blues

I / / / C	I / / / C	I / / / C	I / / / C
IV / / / F	IV / / / F	I / / / C	I / / / C
V / / / G	V / / / G	I / / / C	I / / / C

The next version of the twelve bar blues includes three variations: in the first line, a *IV* chord is inserted to break up the long reign of the *I* chord, a *IV* chord is substituted for the second bar of *V*, and there is now a ***turnaround***.

A turnaround, found in the last bar, strongly propels the listener (and players) back to the top for another go. It also usually involves some kind of rhythmic or textural variation, and features, not surprisingly, the *V* chord. In more complex blues progressions, the turnaround often grows to two bars in length, then filling the eleventh and twelth bar.

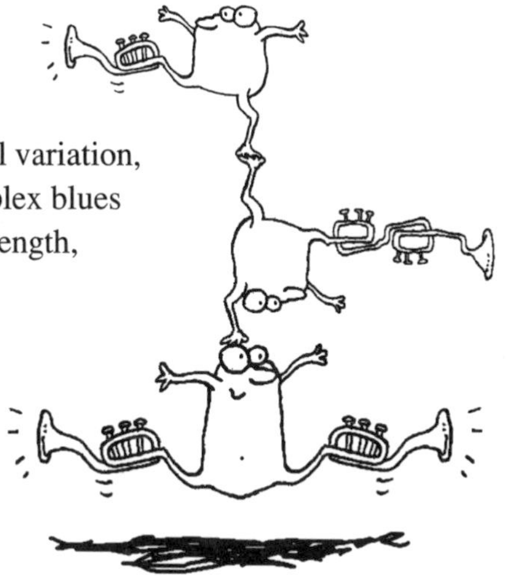

10 You will be formally introduced to these chords in upcoming chapters.

2. basic minimum daily requirement blues

I / / / C	IV / / / F	I / / / C	I(7) / / / C(7)
IV / / / F	IV / / / F	I / / / C	I / / / C
V / / / G	IV / / / F	I / / / C	V / / / G (turnaround)

This second version of the twelve bar blues is perhaps the most prevalent. It is found everywhere in blues, jazz, and rock. It's also a perennial favorite for jam session warm-ups. You'll think of this book next time you go to a jam session: it never fails—after everyone is tuned, there will inevitably be a number of rejected suggestions for a first song until, finally, someone says, "How 'bout we start off with a blues?"

You'll be ready.

3. your own blues

The roots of the blues are preserved in earlier recordings, which are definitely recommended listening for any blues lover. The light they shed on more recent blues is not to be underestimated! Listen to recordings of Willie McTell, Blind Lemon Jefferson, and Robert Johnson. In much of early blues, the meter was anything but strict. Beats and bars were added and omitted freely, according to the whim of the performer. In fact, it could be said that early blues performers felt the music as a flow of beats rather than regular meter and phrase lengths. Today's blues are rigid and predictable in comparison. Again, any blues lover owes it to her/himself to check out early blues recordings. End of lecture.

Chapter 10~ iim, iiim, vim, and vii° Chords... Intro to Chord Substitution

What: The last several chapters introduced you to some uses of the three diatonic major chords, *I*, *IV*, and *V*. Now it's time to examine the remaining four diatonic chords: *iim*, *iiim*, *vim*, and *vii°*. These chords add significant flavor to the diatonic chord palate.

Each of these chords shares two of its three notes with at least one of the diatonic major chords. Chords with notes in common are often interchangeable to some degree. The melody helps to determine chord choice. Basically, the more notes shared by the melody and harmony (chord), the more ***consonant***[11] the sound.

Let's look at some specifics. 𝄞 The *iim* chord shares two of its three notes with the *IV* chord. The *vim* chord shares two-thirds of its notes with *both* the *I* and the *IV* chords, making it a potential substitution candidate for either chord. Similarly, *iiim* shares two of its three notes with both the *I and V* chords, making it a potential candidate for substitution for either of these chords. Finally, the *vii°* chord shares two thirds of its notes with the *V* chord, making these chords interchangeable in many situations. Of the two, the *V* is often chosen over the *vii°* because of its greater *stability* and greater ***consonance***.

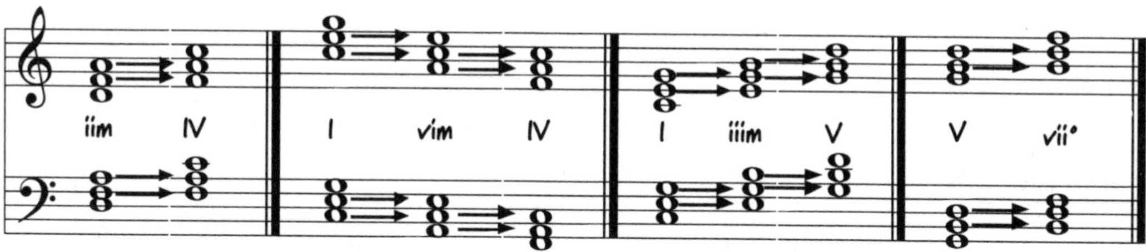

Shared Notes Among Diatonic Chords... Possible Substitute Chords

11 **Consonant** (consonance) means pleasant, resolved, and stable; whereas **dissonant** (**dissonance**) means tense, unresolved, and unstable. These are relative, and depend on context and musical style. What is perceived as consonant in one situation may be perceived as dissonant in another, and vice versa.

Let's go back to our friend Susannah as an example. Here again, is Susannah's rendition of herself from chapter 9: 𝄞

IV I V I V I
Oh, Susannah, don't you cry for me, for I come from Alabama with my banjo on my knee.

Oh Susannah: Tonic, Subdominant, & Dominant Harmony

Now let's give Susannah a little more harmonic interest by adding and substituting some minor diatonic chords for the basic *I*, *IV*, and *V*. Once again, bass cleffers, play any examples that sound muddy 8va (an octave higher). These two Susannahs *definitely* fit into that category. Notating them as I have is merely a case of *ledger-line avoidance*.

IV iim iiim vim iim V iiim vim iim V I
Oh, Susannah, don't you cry for me, for I come from Alabama with my banjo on my knee.

… and, in the key of C: 𝄞

F Dm Em Am Dm G Em Am Dm G C
Oh, Susannah, don't you cry for me, for I come from Alabama with my banjo on my knee.

Oh Susannah: With Diatonic Chord Substitution

Notice the added richness that these new chords impart. Notice also that you can *add* these chords, instead of *substituting* them. The first *iim* is merely added, but the first *iiim* and *vim* instead *replace* the *I* chord, which doesn't appear until the end.

With this latest batch of substitutions, we've begun to stray just enough that some ears may cry out, "But that's not how that song is *supposed* to sound!" Well, so be it. My condolences to the purists; I'm using poor Susannah to drive home some pedagogical points. (Gee, maybe I'd get there faster if I used *pedalogical* [sic] points to ride home. But this is merely shameless, fun word play. Back to work!) Susannah's going to be taken even farther out of her accustomed contexts before she ever gets back home to *I*, *IV*, and *V*… at least in *this* book!

Common Diatonic Progressions Which Include iim, iiim, and vim

Here are some other diatonic chord progressions that show up a lot. The first two show up in zillions of doo-wop songs from the '50s such as "Silhouettes," "Who Wrote the Book of Love," and many others.

‖: I | vim | IV | V :‖

‖: I | vim | iim | V :‖

This next one is *exactly the same chord progression* as the second one above, except that it is offset by two bars. This offset, though, makes its musical meaning different. Play them both, and I think you'll intuitively hear what I mean!

‖: iim | V | I | vim :‖

Chords with notes in common
are often interchangeable to some degree.

The final one is almost the same progression as the one used over and over and over and over and over and over in Pachelbel's canon. The only difference is the second to the last chord is a *IV* instead of a *iim* chord.

‖: I | V | vim | iiim | IV | I | iim | V :‖

There are many combinations and variations; these are just some particularly common ones. Knowing them is a good first step toward being able to pick them out when you hear them.

We'll discuss the roles of these chords in chapter 14.

Chapter 11~
Minor Scales and Keys

The Major's Sad Cousin: the Relative Minor, Your Cousin Alice... and the Natural Minor Scale

What and Why: Every *major* chord, scale, or key has a relative *minor* chord, scale, or key. The concept of relative major and minor allows us to bundle these pairs of related chords, scales, and keys into one parcel for easier carrying just as we bundled seven notes into one major scale. Relative major and minor keys share the same key signature, and are often neighbors in different sections of the same song; frequently even wrestling for control in the same section of a song. I wish *my* relatives[12] were as helpful as the relative minor and relative major relationship.

There is no such thing*, in and of itself,* as a *relative minor chord*, or a *relative major chord*. There is, however, a relative minor of C (A minor), or a relative major of B minor (D major), etc. Think of it like this: your cousin Alice is not *a cousin* in an absolute sense. She *is*, however, *your* cousin. *Cousins* describes the relationship between the two of you, not *what she is* in an absolute sense. Got it?

How: a major chord's relative minor is the minor chord built on the note a major sixth higher than the major chord's root. To find a major chord's relative minor, find the note a major sixth (nine half-steps) higher, and say "minor" after the note.

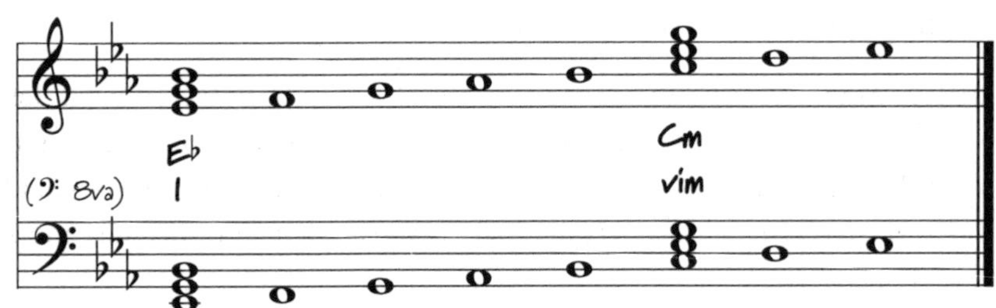

E Flat Major and its Relative Minor, Cm

12 Don't get me wrong; I've got some great relatives.

By the way, each of the diatonic *minor* chords is the relative minor of one of the diatonic *major* chords. Here are examples from the key of C: the *I* chord is C; a major sixth higher is *vim*: Am. The *IV* chord is F; a major sixth higher is *iim*, or Dm. The *V* chord is G, and a major sixth higher is *iiim*, or Em. 𝄞

Diatonic Relative Chords In General and in C

Relative Major	Relative Minor
I (C)	vim (Am)
IV (F)	iim (Dm)
V (G)	iiim (Em)

More Relative Minor and Relative Majors

Here's a spot for you to try your hand at finding the relative minor chord of a major chord, and the relative major of a minor chord. Have fun! A

G ___	B♭ ___	E♭ ___	F# ___
B ___	D ___	A ___	C ___
A♭m ___	E♭m ___	B♭m ___	C#m ___

The Natural Minor Scale

Now that you've been introduced to the relative minor/major *chord* relationship, let's expand that relationship to include *scales* and *keys*.

How: The relative minor key, like the relative minor chord, begins and ends on the sixth note of a major scale. Here's how you find a major key's relative minor key. Find the sixth degree of the major scale. Starting there, play the notes of the major scale all the way 'til you hit the sixth degree one octave higher. Here's an example using the key of C:

1	2	3	4	5	**6**	**7**	**1**	**2**	**3**	**4**	**5**	**6**
C	D	E	F	G	**A**	**B**	**C**	**D**	**E**	**F**	**G**	**A**

There! You just found the relative minor of C major: the key of A minor. The scale itself is a *minor* scale. Minor scales differ from the major scale in that they come in different flavors. That is, there are a handful of them. This one is the *natural minor* scale. 𝄞

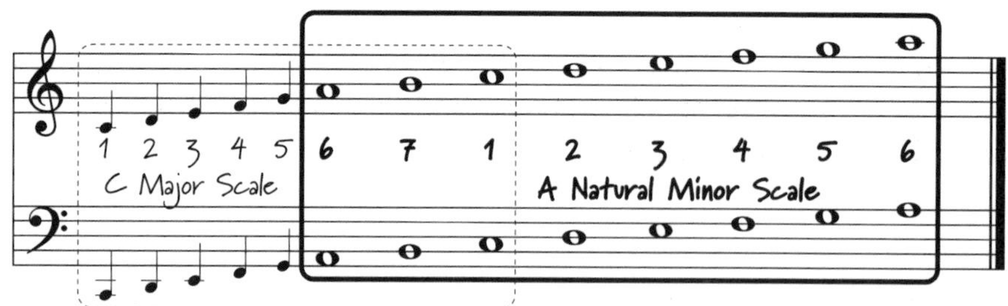

Deriving C Major's Relative Minor Key and Natural Minor Scale (Am)

There's something strangely unsettling, though, about leaving our scale in its current state. Do you feel strangely unsettled? I know I do. I'll tell you why. Scales by definition *begin* and *end* on their tonics. Tonics are home base. Home base ought to be "1," not "6" or another number, don't you think? I'm so glad you agree. What we've done so far is define the natural minor scale only as *a displaced major scale*—that is, a major scale beginning (and ending) on the "wrong" note. Let's redefine it from a different perspective—how it differs from a major scale beginning on the *same* note (***parallel major***[13]), rather than a *different* note (*relative* major).

Using the Major Scale to Define Other Scales

Once you've internalized the major scale pattern (all whole-steps, except half-steps in between three and four, and seven and eight), it can be used for lots of other things, including defining other types of scales, and deriving zillions of chords. The major scale is a handy little devil, that's fer shur!

Here's how the major scale can be used to define other scales: scales other than the major have different patterns of whole-steps and half-steps, but rather than learn a different pattern for each of the many scales, I believe it's easier just to define how the scale *differs* from the major scale. That is, how was the major scale altered in order to arrive at the new scale? Did we lower the third degree a half-step (♭3)? Did we raise the fourth degree a half-step (♯4)?

The flats and sharps in the preceding (and following) examples refer to *modifications of the original major scale*, not actual flats and sharps. For example, if we lower the third degree (♭3) of a D major scale (F♯), it becomes an F♮. If we raise the fourth degree (♯4) of an F major scale (B♭), it becomes a B♮. This is analogous to the way accidentals are used to mean *lowered* or *raised* when defining chords.

13 A major scale's *parallel minor* is the minor key (or natural minor scale) beginning on the same note, as opposed to the *relative minor*, which is the minor key/natural minor scale beginning on the note a major sixth higher. For example, the relative minor of E major is C♯ minor, while the parallel minor of E major is E minor.

Let's get back to our A natural minor scale. This time, compare it not with its relative major, C major, but instead, with its *parallel major*, A major. How was the A major scale changed to make it into an A natural minor scale? It seems that the C# became a C♮, the F# became an F♮, and the G# became a G♮:

A Major Scale	A	B	C#	D	E	F#	G#	A
A Natural Minor Scale	A	B	C	D	E	F	G	A

Now, rephrase that in terms of degrees of the A major scale: the third, sixth, and seventh were lowered, each by a half-step. So, the pattern for the natural minor scale could be summarized as follows:

Natural Minor Scale	1	2	♭3	4	5	♭6	♭7	(8)

This way of describing the natural minor scale ends up being more helpful.

Now we can talk about going back the other direction. Here's how to find the relative major of a minor key: the *relative major* begins on the *(minor) third note of the minor scale*. For example, to find the relative major of F minor, go up a whole step to get to two, and a half-step to get to the lowered third: A♭ is the relative major.

Are you wondering how to tell if a song is in a major key versus a minor key, given that one key signature is shared by both major and minor keys? If so, you aren't alone! The easiest way is to look at the last note of the melody, and the last chord. More often than not, they will both be the tonic of the key: either major or minor! You'll learn an additional way of making this decision very soon.

Just when you thought things were getting simple, here's a monkey wrench for you to chew on—good for the teeth. I mentioned it before, but in case you missed it, here it is again. Unlike the one and only major scale, there is *more than one* minor scale. The natural minor is only *one* of them. Let's now move on to some others.

The Harmonic Minor Scale

One of the strongest forces in Western music is the pull from *V* to *I* (or *V* to *im*). This is *important*, and will come up again and again. For now, notice that if you build a diatonic triad on the fifth degree of the natural minor scale, you get a *minor* triad. This gives us *not V* to *im*, but rather **vm** (a minor dominant) to *im*. This *vm* to *im* sound is good and "minory," but lacks the strong pull of the major dominant to the tonic. The pull of the seventh note to the tonic is much stronger when it's a half-step lower than the tonic (♮7), rather than a whole-step (♭7). The harmonic minor scale lives for a *harmonic* reason: to make the dominant chord major rather than minor. This is done by raising the lowered seventh of the natural minor back to a natural seventh.

Harmonic Minor	1	2	♭3	4	5	♭6	7	(8)
C Harmonic Minor 𝄞	C	D	E♭	F	G	A♭	B	(C)

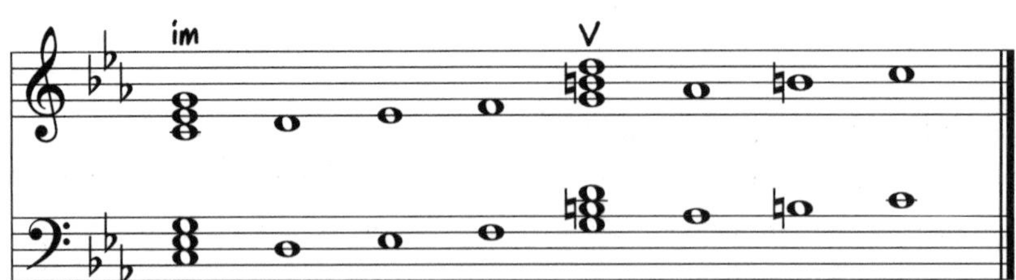

C Harmonic Minor Scale With im and V Chords

The Melodic Minor Scale

The melodic minor scale, as its name implies, exists for melodic reasons. Play the harmonic minor scale, and notice how the jump of a minor third between the ♭6 and ♮7 stands out as being somewhat jagged. You may like it or you may not (I love it!), but I think you'll agree that it's not as smooth as a step from ♭6 to ♭7, or from ♮6 to ♮7. So, to make the harmonic minor scale smoother melodically, without losing the harmonic minor's strong ♮7 to 8 notes and *V* to *im* chords, the ♭6 is raised to a ♮6 in the melodic minor—but only when ascending. When descending, the need for the strong melodic pull from ♮7 to 8 is gone, so the melodic minor is returned to its *natural* state: the *natural* minor scale, complete with ♭6 and ♭7. In this respect, the melodic minor is a unique case in western music; a scale that is different in its ascending and descending forms.

Melodic Minor Scale Pattern and C Melodic Minor Scale 𝄞

1	2	♭3	4	5	6	7	(8)	♭7	♭6	5	4	♭3	2	1
C	D	E♭	F	G	A	B	(C)	B♭	A♭	G	F	E♭	D	C

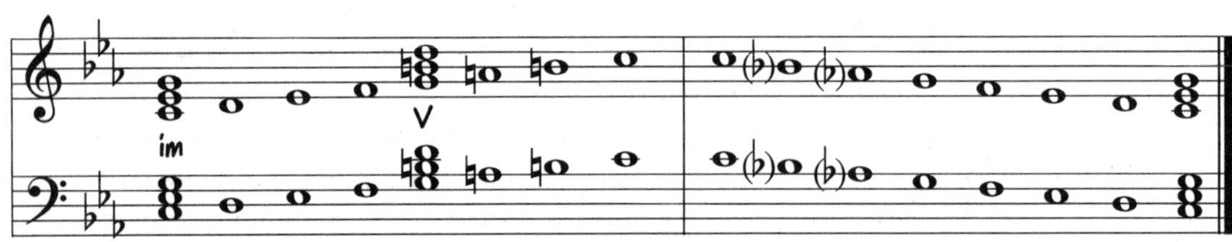

C Melodic Minor Scale—Ascending and Descending

You have learned the Natural Minor, Harmonic Minor, and Melodic Minor scales. Just when you thought you were done, I'll mention that there are *still more* minor scales. Look for some of them in chapter 21.

Chapter 12~ The Circle of Fifths (and Fourths)

Why: Music is full of the same kinds of patterns that you found in your tour of the major scales and keys. It would be helpful to you at this point to have something which visually represents the progression of keys—perhaps a picture of some sort.

What: Enter *the Circle,* a great visual representation of the web of keys and scales. Understand it and be well-rounded. You will take the chart "Major Scales (From Fewest to Most Accidentals)" from chapter 3, and put it into an even more useful form. This more useful form is the Circle. It displays clearly the progression of keys, including the enharmonic keys of B and C♭, C# and D♭, and F# and G♭[14]. It also shows how major and minor chords and scales are related. Before going on, though, I'd suggest you review the scales chart and its accompanying text first.

The circle shows key and chord relationships.

On the next page is a (mostly) blank *Circle* for you to complete. Write the tonics of the major keys on the outside. Continue clockwise on the right through the sharps. On the left, going counterclockwise, continue the flat keys in increasing order. Write each key's correct key signature on the staves (nonreaders can skip this), with the "newest accidental" written next to the staff, as in the example. Write the relative minors in the correct spots on the inner circle. Do as much as you can from memory. I filled in a couple to get you started. A

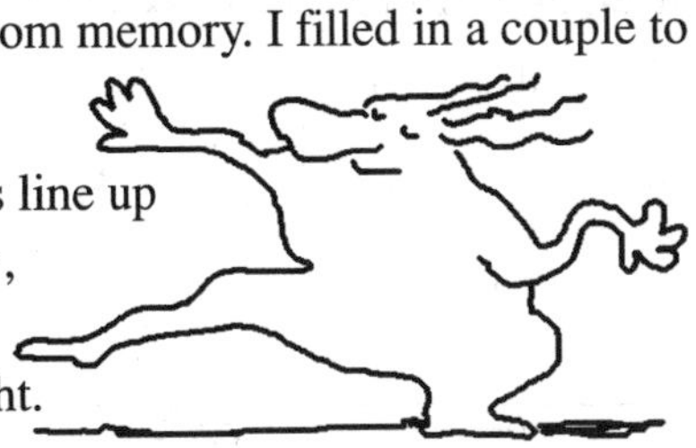

If you do it correctly, the pairs of enharmonic keys line up correctly each with the other. B and C♭, C# and D♭, and F# and G♭ should be in enharmonic pairs. Check the Answers chapter, to see if you got it right.

But first, let me introduce the Circle by its full name: *the Circle of Fifths*. This name alludes to the fact that each tonic is a perfect fifth above the preceding tonic as you move clockwise (more sharps or fewer flats). Now notice that if you move counterclockwise (more flats—fewer sharps), each tonic is a perfect *fourth* above the preceding one. So, to be fair, I'm offering this more complete (and fairer to perfect fourths) name: *The Circle of Fifths (and Fourths).* So there. Joking aside, this is *important* and *useful.* Read it again, if necessary.

---

14 You found these keys to be enharmonic when you initially figured out the major scales, right?

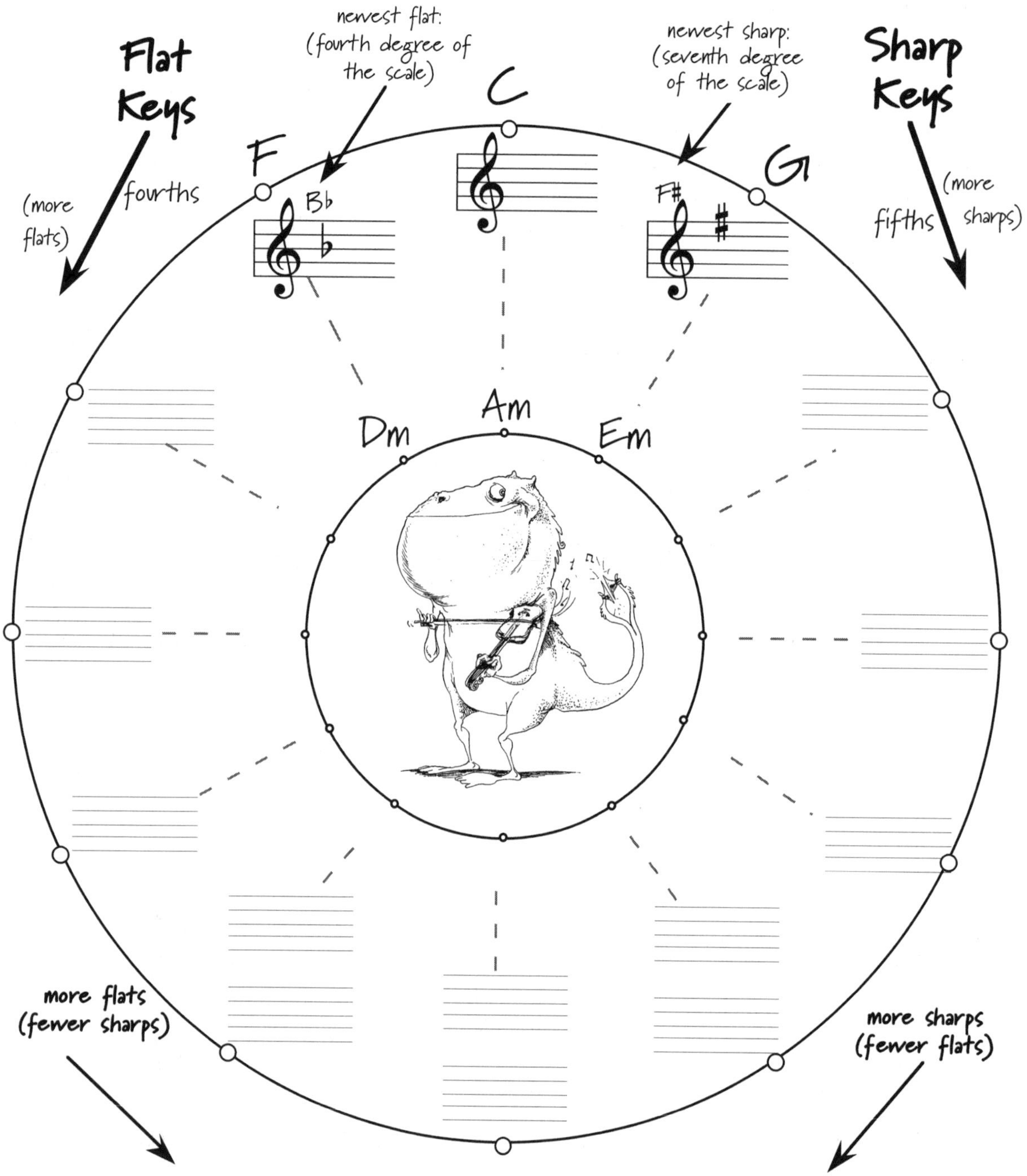

Flat Keys

(more flats)

fourths

newest flat: (fourth degree of the scale)

F

B♭

C

newest sharp: (seventh degree of the scale)

G

F♯

Sharp Keys

(more sharps)

fifths

Dm

Am

Em

more flats (fewer sharps)

more sharps (fewer flats)

The Circle of Fifths (and Fourths)

The Circle... and Keys

Now that you've filled the Circle in, pat yourself on the back. But what can *it* do for *you?*

What: The circle shows keys' relationships to one another. For starters, the closer two keys are on the circle, the more notes they have in common, the more closely related they are musically, and *the more likely they are to be found close together in a musical phrase or piece*. For example, the key of G shares six of its seven notes with its immediate neighbor, the key of C. 𝄞 Shared notes are in **bold** (circled in the illustrations), and tonics are only counted once.

Key of G: **G A B C D E** F# (G)

Key of C: **C D E** F **G A B** (C)

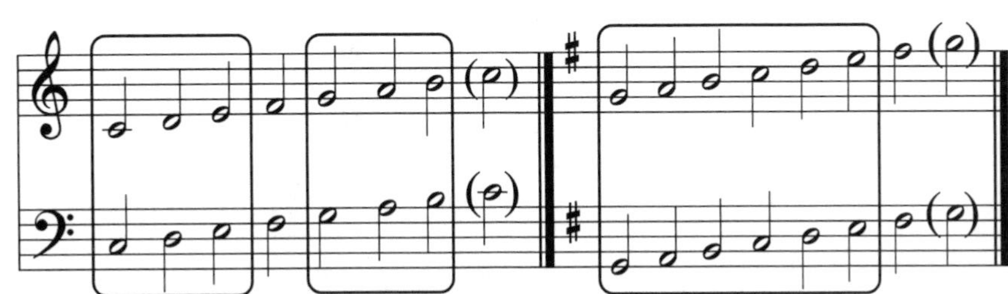

Closely Related Keys of C Major and G Major: Shared Notes

Contrast this with the two notes shared by the key of G and the distant key of A♭. 𝄞

Key of G: **G** A B **C** D E F# G

Key of A♭: A♭ B♭ **C** D♭ E♭ F **G** A♭

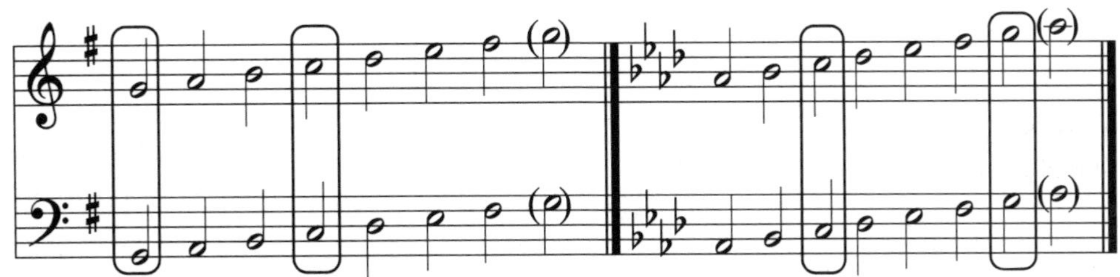

Distantly Related Keys of G Major and A Flat Major: Shared Notes

Although the *notes* G and A♭ are very close to one another (a half-step away), the *keys* are very distant in that they only share two notes in common! Therefore, a transition between the keys of G and A♭ would be more abrupt than a transition between the keys of G and C or D. More generally, the more notes which two keys share, the smoother the transition between those two keys. Composers use this phenomenon, consciously or not, when writing music. When a composer wants to change the musical palette gently, the key changes to a closely related key. *This isn't always what is desired* at a given point in a piece or song, though. So often, you'll find that a song will change to a distant key for a totally fresh and new sound… or to jolt the listener awake.

The Circle... and Chords

Now, think of what you filled in on the Circle as *chords* rather than scales. Yep. Handy li'l bugger that it is, the Circle also shows *chord* relationships. For starters, chords that are close together on the circle are commonly seen and heard together in many kinds of music. Chords far from eachother on the circle will be rarely found close together in music. They sound much less natural in succession. Try it, and you'll see for yourself. Try repeating a bar of a C chord and a bar of an F# chord several times. The progression is abrupt and somewhat disorienting. Compare this to a bar of C alternating with a bar of F or G chords. Either of these will sound natural and familiar in comparison.

Let's get specific. Any three adjacent major chords on the circle are *IV, I,* and *V* for the key in the middle. That is, any *I* chord is flanked by its *IV* on the counterclockwise side, and its *V* on the clockwise side. For instance, E♭ (*I*) is surrounded by A♭ (*IV*) and B♭ (*V*), while in the following diagram, C (*I*) is surrounded by F (*IV*) and G (*V*).

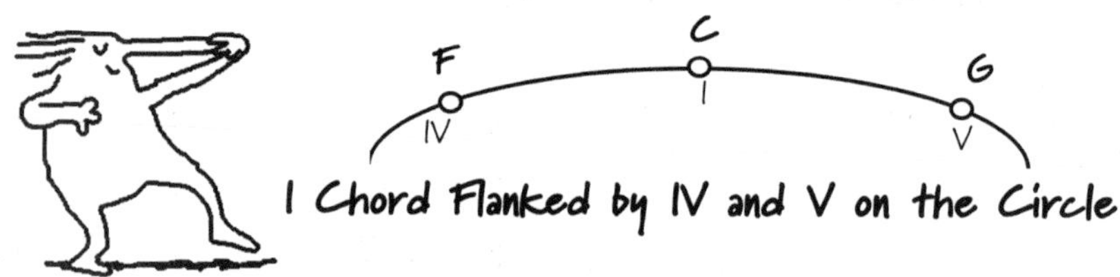

I Chord Flanked by IV and V on the Circle

In fact, this business of related chords on the circle can be taken further to include the relative minors from the inner circle. They are the the diatonic minor chords for the major in the middle. For example, six of the seven diatonic chords in the key of C are clustered around C at 12:00 on the circle: C, Dm, Em, F, G, and Am. (Missing is the diminished chord built on the seventh degree—no surprise given that there's no space on the circle devoted to diminished chords.) Again, don't take my word for it; look for yourself!

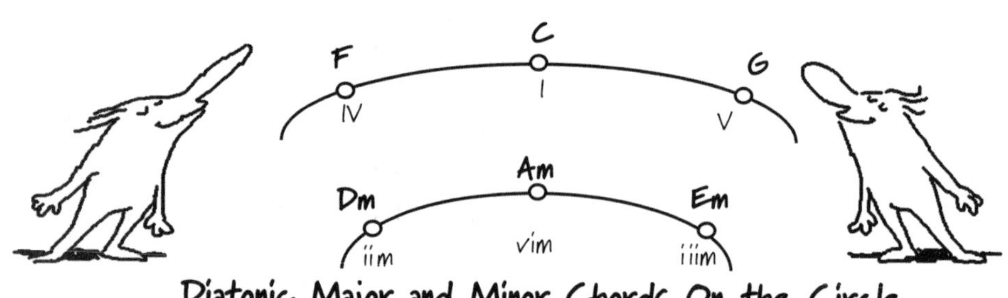

Diatonic Major and Minor Chords On the Circle

See? There are all the chords from the previous version of "Oh Susannah."

F Dm Em Am Dm G Em Am Dm G C
Oh, Susannah, don't you cry for me, for I come from Alabama with my banjo on my knee.

I'll close this chapter with this little tidbit. As with the majors on the outer ring, notice that any three adjacent *minor* chords on the inner ring are *ivm, im,* and *vm* for the *minor* key in the middle. That is, any *i* chord is flanked by its *ivm* on the counterclockwise side, and its *vm* on the clockwise side. Ahhh, the Circle. I think it's great.

Chapter 13~ Chords: 7ths (& 6ths)

What: Four-note chords include various *seventh chords* (seventh, major seventh, minor seventh, and so on), and two *sixth chords* (sixth and minor sixth).

How: To make seventh chords, simply add a seventh, or lowered seventh, to the three notes which make up a triad. You could also think of this as throwing yet another third onto the triadic stack. To make either of the two *sixth chords*, you add a sixth instead of a seventh.

Seventh (& Sixth) Chords

NAME (CHORD TYPE)	ABBREVIATION	SPELLING				C SAMPLE 𝄞			
major 7th	maj^7, Δ^7, M^7	1	3	5	7	C	E	G	B
(dominant) 7th	^{7}	1	3	5	♭7	C	E	G	B♭
minor 7th	m^7, -^{7}	1	♭3	5	♭7	C	E♭	G	B♭
7th, flat 5	$^{7\flat5}$	1	3	♭5	♭7	C	E	G♭	B♭
minor 7th flat 5 ❖	m$^{7\flat5}$, -$^{7\flat5}$	1	♭3	♭5	♭7	C	E♭	G♭	B♭
diminished 7th	$^{\circ7}$, dim^7	1	♭3	♭5	𝄫7 (=6)	C	E♭	G♭	A
augmented 7th	+^{7}, aug^7	1	3	#5	♭7	C	E	G#	B♭
suspended 7th	sus^7	1	4	5	♭7	C	F	G	B♭
sixth	6	1	3	5	6	C	E	G	A
minor sixth	m^6, –^{6}	1	♭3	5	6	C	E♭	G	A
minor, major 7th	– (maj^7), m^{M7}	1	♭3	5	7	C	E♭	G	B
major 7 flat 5	maj$^{7\flat5}$, M$^{7\flat5}$	1	3	♭5	7	C	E	G♭	B
aug. major 7th	maj^7+, M^7+	1	3	#5	7	C	E	G#	B

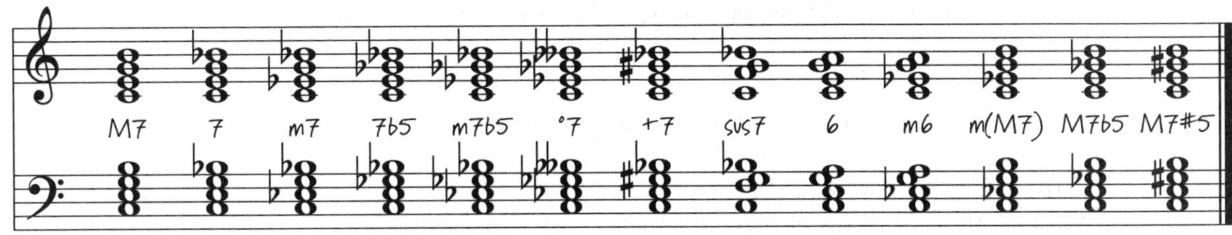

Seventh (& Sixth) Chords Built on C

❖ The m7♭5 chord is often called a half-diminished seventh and abbreviated "ø7," and sometimes even merely "ø."

- Seventh chords use a lowered seventh (♭7th) unless a major seventh is specified.

  Examples: D^7 versus DM^7 $B\flat^7$ versus $B\flat maj^7$ F^7 or Fm^7 versus $F^{\Delta 7}$

- Of the chords you have just learned, dominant seventh chords are especially important players! For now, just keep this in mind… or don't. Either way, it will be back.

- In jazz, the dominant seventh chord is often boiled down to its most important chord-tones; 1, 3, and ♭7. This is done to enable other chord extensions (9ths, 11ths, and 13ths) and alterations ($\#^5$, $\flat^5$, etc.) to be added more freely. This will come up again.

Contemporary Chord Nomenclature Pep Talk

Now that you've learned seventh (and sixth) chords, it's time for a quick speech in support of the chord nomenclature (lingo) you've been learning. Chords will almost *double in size* from our beloved sevenths (and sixths) before this book is done, and names such as "major seventh, flat five" or "minor, major seventh" may already seem unwieldy. Yet, it is worth it. Here are several reasons why.

The first one has to do with the fact that our harmonic lingo *evolved* over time. It was not invented all of the sudden. As musical harmony became more complex, chord names, out of necessity, did the same. Notes that were initially thought of as temporary visitors to chords, such as a suspended fourth, moved in as permanent parts of chords, and hence became part of the chord's name. As chords grew in size from three to six or more notes, their names by necessity became more complicated. Like it or not, this is the way chords are commonly spoken of in our culture. The more you use these chords, and their names, the more the names will become second nature to you.

Second, in contemporary popular styles (jazz, blues, rock, and all their offshoots), the *general note content* of a chord is usually considerably more important than specifics such as octave, ***inversion, chord-tone doubling***, and ***voicing***. These are generally left up to the tastes and preferences of the performer—of course, within the dictates of common practice. The system of nomenclature that you're in the process of learning, though sometimes unwieldy, provides the necessary information while avoiding the rest.

Finally, these names put the notes into one easy-to-deal-with package. Convenient just like folks prefer nowadays. This package clearly shows a chord's *quality* or *type*, even when ***transposed*** into another key. For example, it's easy to see that $Dmaj^{7\flat 5}$ and $Fmaj^{7\flat 5}$ are the same type of chord built on different roots. The name "$maj^{7\flat 5}$" makes it clear. This similarity is less obvious from looking only at the notes that make up each chord: D, F#, A♭, C#, and F, A, C♭, E, respectively.

Yaaaay, contemporary chord nomenclature!

Triad, Seventh, and Sixth Chord Practice

Try your hand at building these chords. This calls into play your knowledge of major scales, as well as the chord construction covered above. Try constructing the necessary scales from memory instead of looking back at the scales you've already constructed. There is blank staff paper on the following page for the readers among you.

Fmaj7 F A C E..........

A♭7 ....

B♭m7 ....

F♯ ....

Dm7♭5 ....

Em (maj7)..........

G♭ ....

A+7 ....

D♭m ....

Bmaj7+ ....

E♭m6 ....

D sus ....

Cm7♭5 ....

G sus ....

F+ ....

D♭+ ....

A+ ....

D7 ....

Asus7 ....

G°7 ....

E°7 ....

B♭°7 ....

D♭°7 ....

Am7♭5 ....

A♭m ....

Dmaj7 ....

E♭+ ....

F♯6 ....

E♭m7 ....

AM7♭5 ....

E7 ....

F7♭5 ....

F♯ ....

Dm6 ....

G♯m ....

B♭m (maj7)..........

C♯m7♭5 ....

Triad, Seventh, and Sixth Chord Practice: Notation

Symmetrical Chords and Functions

When you were building the chords in the workbook exercises, you may have noticed that the consecutive augmented chords were all made up of the same notes. The same was true of the consecutive diminished seventh chords. It turns out that *augmented triads* and *diminished sevenths* are *symmetrical*: this means that each chord is made up of only one type of interval; major thirds in the case of the augmented triad, and minor thirds in the case of the diminished seventh (°7).

For example, a B♭°7 chord is B♭, D♭, F♭, A𝄫 (or more colloquially: B♭, D♭, E, G). To see that we have *all* stacked minor thirds, we must *double the root*—add another B♭ root on top of the stack: B♭, D♭, E, G, B♭—there, all (enharmonic) minor thirds! 𝄞

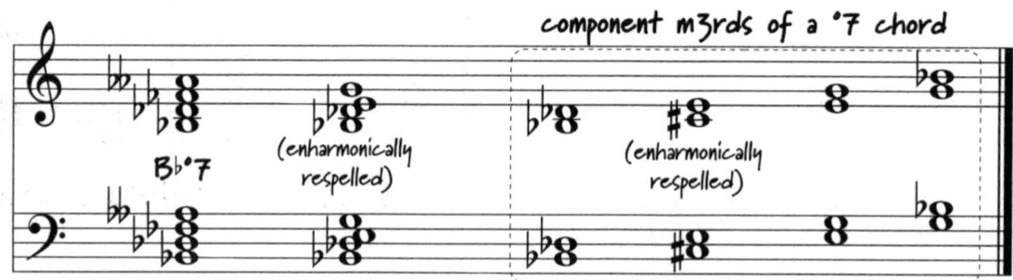

Symmetrical Nature of the °7 Chord: Stacked Minor Thirds

Notice also that if we take the chord apart, we can also see that it contains not one, but two ***tritones***[15]: B♭ to E, and D♭ to G… and their respective inversions. Pack this fact away in your brain for a rainy day! 𝄞

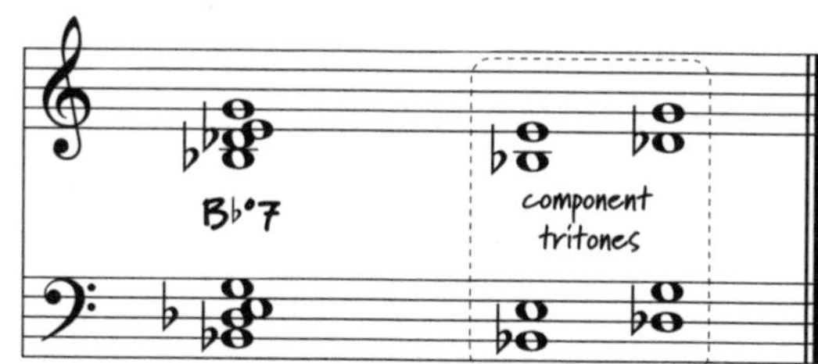

Return of the Symmetrical Nature of the °7 Chord: Component Tritones

An F+ chord is F, A, C#. Throw another F root on *top* of the stack (F, A, C#, F), and you have a chord constructed of only (enharmonic) major thirds. 𝄞

Symmetrical Nature of the Augmented Chord: Stacked Major Thirds

In both cases, some enharmonic respelling is necessary in order for the thirds to be spelled correctly. That is, in the case of the F+, it's easier to see that C# to F sounds like a major third if it's respelled D♭ to F, so it also *looks* like a major third!

So what: In practical use, this means three things: first, that any symmetrical chord has as many names as it has notes (for example, B♭°7 = D♭°7 = E°7 = G°7, and F+ = A+ = C#+ = F+). Second, *any* note of a symmetrical chord can act as the root. Which note ends up being blessed with the distinction depends on context and smooth bass movement. Third, due to their symmetry, a diminished seventh or augmented chord can lead to any of several chords. Composers have taken advantage of this fact for centuries.

In terms of what we hear, diminished seventh and augmented chords' symmetry makes them unstable—our ears want them to *resolve* to a more stable chord such as a major or minor. A song that ended on a diminished seventh or augmented chord would sound unfinished at best. The listener would expect a stable chord before being convinced the song were indeed done. Try it; you'll see what I mean.

---

15 As a reminder, two notes a distance of three whole-steps apart (C to F# or Bb to E, for example) form the interval of a **tritone** (meaning "three notes…" apart). The tritone is a particularly dissonant interval.

Again, diminished and augmented chords, and unstable chords in general, act mostly as *passing* chords. This is doubly true for diminished seventh chords. They act like magnets, pulling one chord to another. Try playing these examples, and listen for the unstable sound of these chords. 𝄞

| C | C#$^{\circ 7}$ | Dm^7 | D#$^{\circ 7}$ | Em^7 | B$^{\circ 7}$ | C ||

| C | C+ | F | A+ | Dm | G+ | C ||

C C#°7 Dm7 D#°7 Em7 B°7 C

A Progression Using Diminished Seventh Passing Chords

Diminished and augmented chords, and unstable chords in general, act mostly as **passing** chords.

C C+ F A+ Dm G+ C

A Progression Using Augmented Passing Chords

Chapter 14~ Diatonic Chords and Functions

Diatonic Seventh Chords

In order to get an accurate picture of diatonic chord functions, you must know the diatonic sevenths as well as the diatonic triads. Now that you're comfortable constructing sevenths, write the correct names for each diatonic chord in the blank row in the chart and notation example. The pattern of diatonic seventh chords is nestled in the Answers chapter, should you need it.

Diatonic Seventh Chords Chart

Name	Tonic	Supertonic	Mediant	Subdom.	Dominant	Submediant	Leading Tone
Scale Degree	1	2	3	4	5	6	7
Seventh	B	C	D	E	F	G	A
Fifth	G	A	B	C	D	E	F
Third	E	F	G	A	B	C	D
Root	C	D	E	F	G	A	B
7th Chord	CM7						

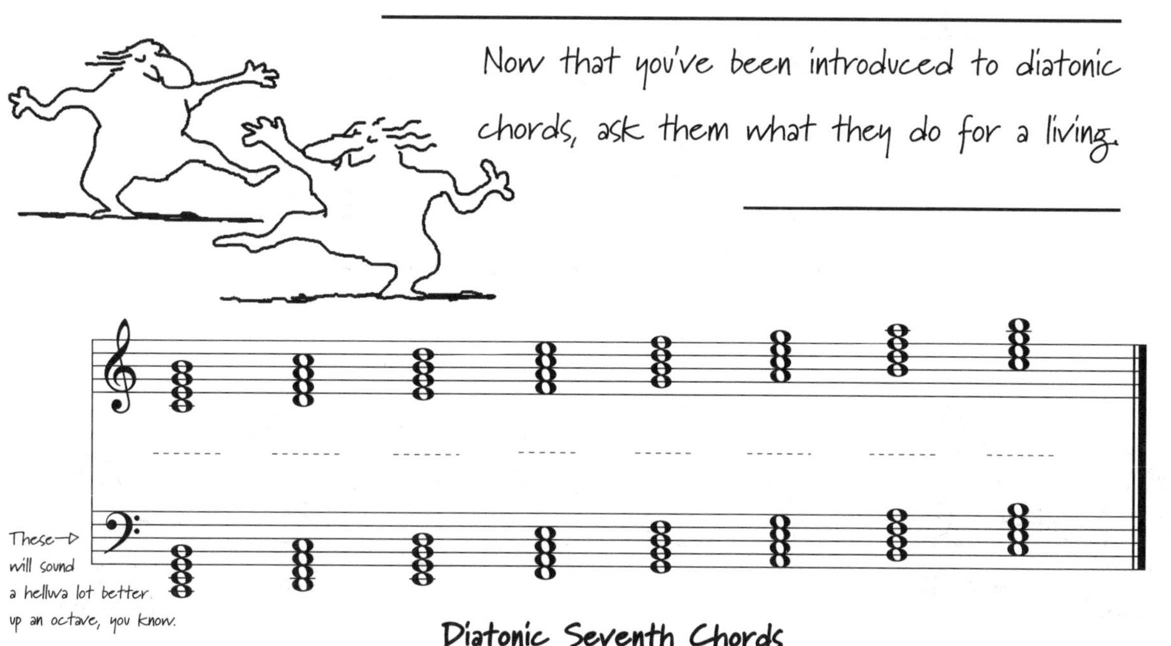

Diatonic Seventh Chords

Diatonic Chord Functions in Major Keys

Why: Now that you've been introduced to diatonic triads and sevenths, it's time to ask them what they do for a living. It's polite at least, and at most will definitely help you on your way toward musical enlightenment. I'll talk about chord *families*, which can include triads and their various extensions (sevenths, as well as ninths and other chords you will soon learn). Let's begin.

The tonic (I) chord family (including upward extensions, especially sevenths and ninths—to be explained soon) is musical home base, resolution, comfort, and finality (and very often, starting point too)—like a pendulum at rest. It is where the music lands when gravity has done all that it can. It is the only chord (family) with which modal or tonal music can sound truly finished.

The dominant (V) chord (and chord *family*, again, including higher extensions) is musical homesickness, restlessness, tension, and expectation—a wound-up spring. It is just *dying* to resolve back to the tonic (one notch counter-clockwise on the Circle). Of course, it doesn't *always*, or things would become boring, but this is its foremost role. Here's a *grandiose proclamation:* the most significant driving force in Western music is the relationship between the *tonic* and *dominant*. This is a small paragraph, but if you were to remember only one thing from this book, let this be it.

The V7 Chord is by far the most important of the diatonic sevenths. It is a dominant seventh built on the dominant (fifth note of the scale). Notice that the third and lowered seventh of the dominant seventh chord form a tritone interval. The instability of the tritone gives dominant seventh chords (whether built on the dominant (*V*), or not) their characteristic inclination to resolve—to move the harmony toward their tonic home.

The pull from dominant to tonic is even stronger when the dominant is a seventh rather than a triad. The seventh chord built on the dominant (fifth degree) is the *only diatonic dominant seventh chord*. This, in fact, is the source of the name *dominant seventh*. *Dominate,* it does, though not as much as the tonic. Analyze any song in almost any style, and you will without a doubt find more tonic and dominant chords than any others.

Dominant Seventh Chord and Its Tritone

The subdominant's (IV) role is the first to be less clearly defined. It shares the feeling of "away-ness" of the dominant, although to a much lesser degree. It sometimes feels like a predecessor to the dominant—a *predominant*, if you will. 𝄞

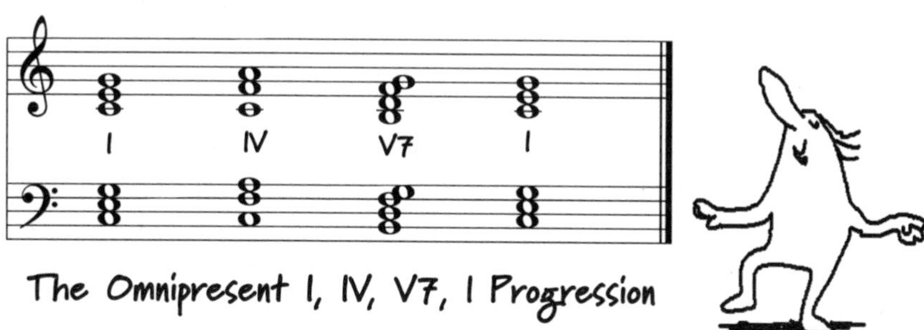

The Omnipresent I, IV, V7, I Progression

The supertonic (iim) triad is also often found preceding the dominant chord. In fact, the *iim*^{7}, *V*^{7} progression ("two-five," as it's commonly known)—sometimes followed by the tonic chord ("two-five-one")—is probably the most important progression in jazz. 𝄞

Jazz's Favorite: the iim7, V7, I

The mediant (iiim) and **submediant (vim)** chords' roles are even less clearly defined. They tend to duplicate the functions of their respective relative majors, but subserviently so, and of course, with a certain minor flavor (see chapter 10).

The leading tone or **subtonic (vii°)** generally duplicates the functions of the dominant, given that its three notes are all contained in the *V*^{7} chord. Being a diminished triad, though, it is heard less frequently. Both chords contain the unstable *tritone*. For example, in the key of C, the *vii°* chord is B° (B, D, F). The *V*^{7} is G^7 (G, B, D, F). 𝄞

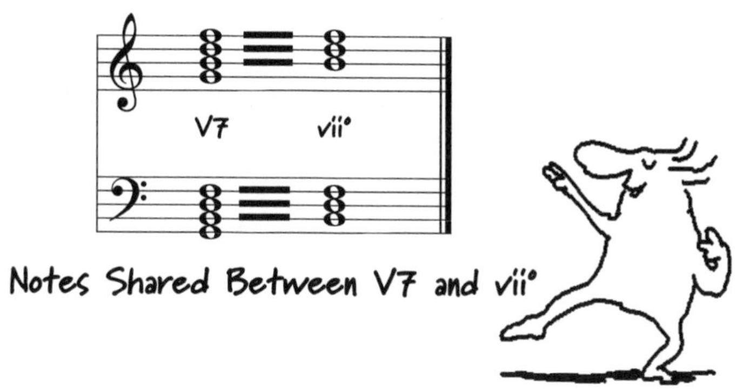

Notes Shared Between V7 and vii°

As I said earlier, these are the chords' most common roles. Happily, they also have minds of their own, and do not always go where expected. Don't take my word for it, though. As you play and listen, notice how chords behave—and misbehave.

The last time we saw Susannah, she was happily dressed in diatonic triads. Now, she is oh so thrilled to be played with diatonic seventh chords that she'll stop crying and begin to swoon… banjo or no banjo (𝄢 8va—up an octave, please):

IV iim^7 iiim^7 vim iim^7 V^7 iiim^7 vim^7 iim^7 V^7 I^6
Oh, Susannah, don't you cry for me, for I come from Alabama with my banjo on my knee.

… and, in the key of C: 𝄞

F Dm^7 Em^7 Am Dm^7 G^7 Em^7 Am^7 Dm^7 G^7 C^6
Oh, Susannah, don't you cry for me, for I come from Alabama with my banjo on my knee.

Oh Susannah: With Diatonic Seventh Chords

Diatonic Chord Functions in Minor Keys

In minor keys, the roles of the tonic, subdominant, and submediant are similar to their roles in major. Some other things change, though…

The mediant chord of the minor scale is now the highly charismatic, VIC (Very Important Chord) (fanfare, please!) relative major. The relative major is ready and able at any time to usurp the reign of the minor tonic, and take over the role of tonic. If and when it does, the music has ***modulated*** (changed key)—whether temporarily or permanently—into the key of the relative major.

The dominant chord still dominates, but something has changed. In the case of the natural minor scale, the dominant chord is now minor, and has a considerably weaker pull towards the tonic. To rectify this questionably lamentable state of affairs, the "*vm*" and "*vm*^{7}" chords are often transformed into the more magnetic "*V*" and "*V*^{7}" chords, by raising the seventh degree of the scale. This, by the way, is usually said to be the origin of the aptly named harmonic minor scale.

At the end of each verse of the well-known folk tune, "Greensleeves" (the Christmas carol "What Child is This"), the V^7 makes an appearance. (The sixth and seventh degrees of the scale are also raised, imparting a melodic minor flavor.) 𝄞

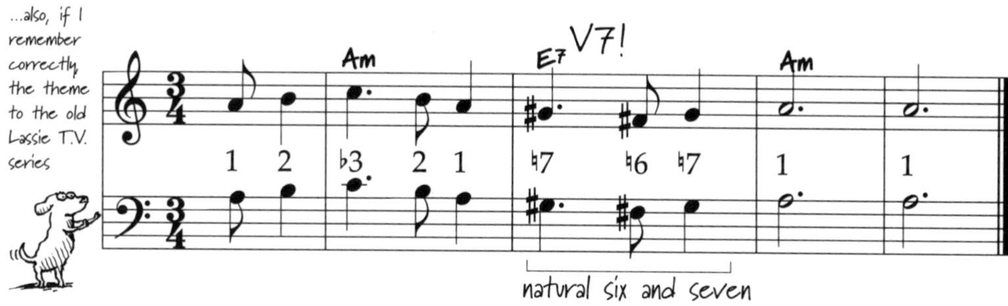

Greensleeves: Use of the V7 in a Minor Key

Chords with a nondiatonic root are analyzed similarly to nondiatonic notes. For example, in the key of C, an E♭ note is ♭3. An E♭ *chord* in the key of C is ♭*III*. An F# note in C is #4, and an F#m$^{7\flat5}$ would be #*ivm*$^{7\flat5}$.

The ♭VII chord pulls as much or more to the *relative major* as it does to the minor tonic. This is because it is the *V* chord of the relative major (♭*III*), and you remember that "five to one) is a *very, very* important chord progression. The following example in the key of A minor shows the G chord serving both roles. 𝄞 The first G chord sits neatly in the key as ♭*VII*. The second one acts as a "five of (flat) three," or *V*/♭*III*, the dominant of the C chord that follows. (This is known as a *secondary dominant*, covered more in chapter 17.) This function is perhaps this chord's most important role in minor keys.

When used with Roman numerals, a slash (/) generally means "of."

im V im bVII im V/bIII bIII

G Chord Serving a Dual Role as bVII and V/bIII Chords in the Key of Am

Chapter 15~ Interval Inversion

What happens when intervals stand on their heads? It's ***inversion***, just as it is when we stand on *our* heads! Yes, intervals are people too.

Why **bother** inverting intervals?

How do you invert an interval? Just lower the top note by one octave, *or* raise the bottom note by one octave… the same interval results either way. The only difference is that the resulting inverted interval will be an *octave higher* using the second method. For example, if we invert the perfect fifth of E up to B, we get the perfect fourth of B up to E. 𝄞

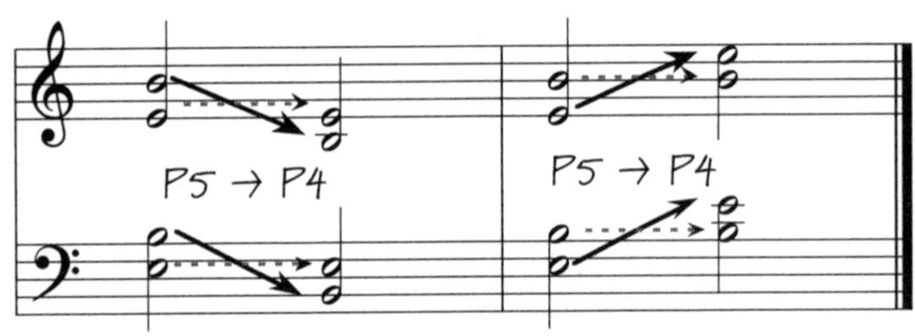

Interval Inversion

Whether or not you realize it, you've already had experience inverting intervals in chapter 6. The thirds and sixths you used to harmonize a major scale are *inversions of each other*, as are the perfect fourths and perfect fifths in the example above.

Why *bother* inverting intervals? There are many reasons. Intervals that invert to each other, such as the perfect fourth and fifth, share similar general sound characteristics. Understanding interval inversion will help immensely in getting around scales, keys, and very importantly, on *your instrument*. Having said that, I'll add that you probably won't *need* interval inversion immediately. Their significance will dawn on you gradually as you study, play, and write music. If interval inversion makes sense to you, or merely intrigues you, work with it for a while. If not, skip this chapter and come back someday. When you need it, it's here. Otherwise, plunge—or plod—on.

Interval Inversion Summaries

I don't generally care much for formulas, but in case you do, this particular formula works to figure the inversion *number*, but not the *quality* (major, minor, etc.):

nine minus the interval number = the inverted interval number.
(9 - interval number = inverted interval number)

For example: A third inverts to what? Nine minus three equals six, therefore a third inverts to a sixth. A to C is a third; C to A is a sixth.

How do you invert an interval? Just lower the top note by one octave, or raise the bottom note by one octave.

All intervals of a certain quality always invert to a specific quality (*major* intervals always invert to a *minor* interval, for instance). Only *perfect intervals* invert to the *same* quality (a perfect interval). All others invert to a different quality (*diminished* intervals invert to *augmented* intervals).

Similarly, interval numbers always invert to specific interval numbers (thirds always invert to sixths, seconds to sevenths, etc.). These are both worth knowing.

I prefer getting to know the inversions gradually over using a formula. Either way, here are two charts. The one on the left deals with the general interval *quality*, and the one on the right deals with the general interval *number*, or the *size* of the interval.

Interval Inversion Charts

Interval type	<–Inverts To–>	Interval Type
perfect	..............<—>..............	perfect
major	..............<—>..............	minor
minor	..............<—>..............	major
tritone	..............<—>..............	tritone
diminished	...........<—>...........	augmented
augmented	...........<—>...........	diminished

Interval	<–Inverts To–>	Interval
unison	..............<—>..............	octave
2nd	..............<—>..............	7th
3rd	..............<—>..............	6th
4th	..............<—>..............	5th
5th	..............<—>..............	4th
6th	..............<—>..............	3rd
7th	..............<—>..............	2nd
octave	..............<—>..............	unison

Ok, chart-heads, let me combine the two preceding charts especially for you, and add examples starting on C. We'll get yet another chart. Yippee! 𝄞

Specific Chromatic Interval Inversion

C Example	Interval	<–Inverts To–>	Interval	C Example
C - C	perfect octave	<—>	perfect unison	C - C
C - B	major seventh	<—>	minor second	B - C
C - B♭	minor seventh	<—>	major second	B♭ - C
C - A	major sixth	<—>	minor third	A - C
C - A♭	minor sixth	<—>	major third	A♭ - C
C - G	perfect fifth	<—>	perfect fourth	G - C
C - G♭	diminished fifth (tritone)	<—>	augmented fourth (tritone)	G♭ - C
C - F#	augmented fourth (tritone)	<—>	diminished fifth (tritone)	F# - C
C - F	perfect fourth	<—>	perfect fifth	F - C
C - E	major third	<—>	minor sixth	E - C
C - E♭	minor third	<—>	major sixth	E♭ - C
C - D	major second	<—>	minor seventh	D - C
C - D♭	minor second	<—>	major seventh	D♭ - C
C - C	perfect unison	<—>	perfect octave	C - C

Chromatic Interval Inversion

Chapter 16~ Intervals for Ear-Training

By now, you're a long time pal of intervals, both right-side-up and upside-down. How 'bout some help learning the sound of each one?

Why: Associating a familiar melody with each interval is a quick way to learn an interval's distinct sound. Soon, you'll no longer need this crutch, but it's a handy one while you *do* need it. I remember when I was in seventh grade (or was it ninth?), Mr. Rondina taught me this approach to hearing intervals while munching his sandwich during his lunch period. Thanks, Mr. Rondina!! I'm forever grateful. By the way, can I call you Carl now?

The tough thing about listing songs for each interval is that different people from different generations and regions know different songs! I've tried to pick as many commonly known songs as possible. If these don't do it for you, find songs that *you* know which begin with these intervals. Go on, it'll be an excellent exercise. Send your results to me, and I'll include them in the next edition of this book. Your name will automatically be entered in the *Friends of Ear-Training Hall of Fame*.

Intervals are people too.

A melodic interval can be *ascending or descending*. Either way, it's still the same interval. Don't confuse this with interval *inversion*. A minor third is still a minor third, no matter which note comes first.

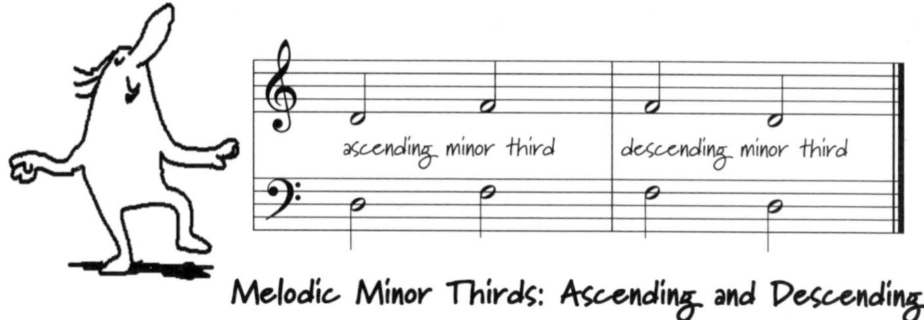

Melodic Minor Thirds: Ascending and Descending

In the following chart, the interval in question consists of the first two *different* notes of the song unless otherwise noted. (Sometimes, the interval is the first and third notes. Ignore repeated first notes, such as the first two notes of "Twinkle Twinkle.")

Intervals diatonic to the major scale are again pointed out (☞).

Interval Reference-Tune Chart

☞ P Octave.....Somewhere Over the Rainbow/Take Me Out to the Ball Game

☞ M7.............Bali Hai, Over the Rainbow (first and third notes in both cases)

m7 ....original Star Trek TV theme, There's a Place for Us

☞ M6.............My Bonnie, Crazy, old NBC notes, It Came Upon a Midnight Clear

m6 ....Black Orpheus, Love Story

☞ P5 ....Twinkle Twinkle, God Rest Ye Merry Gentlemen, Feelings, Chim Chim Cheree

º5 (+4)........Maria ("…I just met a girl named Maria")

☞ P4 ....Here Comes the Bride, Auld Lang Syne, Hark the Herald Angels, Oh Christmas Tree, We Wish You a Merry Christmas

☞ M3.............Oh Susannah (chorus), Morning has Broken, Marine's Hymn, Westminster Chimes, Beethoven's Fifth Symphony

m3 ....Sounds of Silence, What Child is This, Star Spangled Banner, Dixie, Santa Claus is Coming, Oh Holy Night, Angels We Have Heard On High

☞ M2.............I'm a Little Teapot, Silent Night, Deck the Halls, Three Blind Mice

m2 ....Für Elise, Joy To the World,

☞ P Unison.....(oh, come on… you know what this sounds like!)

General Sound of Various Intervals

Now that we've taken a close-up look at the intervals, let's take a gentle step backwards to categorize them according to their sound. Intervals can be classified generally as ***consonant*** or ***dissonant***[16], although context and musical style can be an important factor in determining consonance and dissonance. (It's easier to hear the consonance or dissonance of *harmonic* intervals than *melodic* ones. Play these intervals harmonically if possible.)

Here is a list showing the relative stability (consonance) or instability (dissonance) of the intervals up to an octave. Beyond the octave, the intervals pretty much share the general characteristics of their corresponding "less than an octave" counterparts. See if you can hear the relative consonance or dissonance of each one.

Consonant (stable): Perfect unison, m3, M3, P4, P5, m6, M6, P octave.

Dissonant (unstable): m2, M2, +4 (°5), m7, M7

Another gentle step away will give us a perspective to summarize the sound of the consonant intervals in yet more subjective terms, as follows: *Hollow* sounds comparatively austere and earthy, reminiscent of Gregorian chant, Indian drones and Scottish bagpipes… and heavy metal rhythm guitar. *Sweet* intervals sound more flowery and pretty.

"Hollow": Perfect unison**,** P4, P5, P octave. (perfect intervals and their inversions)

"Sweet": m3, M3, m6, M6. (thirds and sixths)

Here you see one practical application of interval inversion: an interval shares its basic subjective sound quality (*sweet* versus *hollow*) with its inversion.

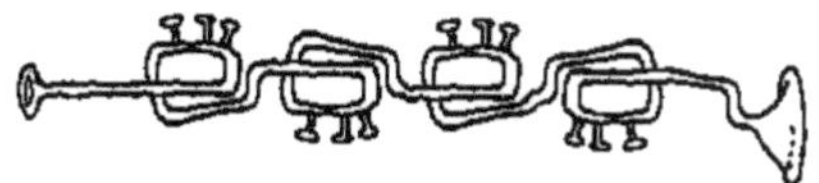

Ear-Training Methods

How do you take this information on the road? There's the high (tech) road—computer, or the low (tech) road—friend. The high-tech road is discussed in chapter 30. This is the low-tech section. Have your friend give you *active* and *passive* ear-training drills. *Active* could be having your friend play a note and ask you to sing another note, i.e.,"I'm playing A♭ one octave below middle C. Sing D above middle C." Another: your friend would play a note and ask you to sing some *interval* above or below. A *passive* drill would be something like: "I'm going to play two notes in succession. Tell me the interval," or, "I'm playing an E♭ two octaves above middle C. Name this next note." Harmonic intervals can also be drilled this way. ("I'm playing two notes. What is the interval?" or, "I'm playing two notes; the bottom (or top) one is the G below middle C. What is the second note?") These types of drills can also be done with chords, chord progressions, etc. Working with a partner is fun, flexible, and low in fat… and it's *free*. Computers cost more than friends, but basically do the same thing… without ever getting bored.

16 Beginning music students usually equate "dissonant" with "bad sounding" and "consonant" with "good sounding," respectively. While there is some truth in these definitions, they don't go far enough. **Dissonance and consonance** mean **tension and resolution**, or **instability and stability**. They are fundamental motivating aspects of music. They are also **relative** rather than **absolute**, and depend on the context and musical style. A dominant seventh chord may have a dissonant effect in Mozart, but will come across as very consonant in a blues, or in a Stravinsky piece.

Chapter 17~
Secondary Dominants and Other Secondary Chords

Why: Up to now, it's been sufficient to name chords simply according to where they occur in a key. That shows where they live, but doesn't address what they do for a living. Let's look one level deeper, and where relevant, name chords by how they *function*. This will come up the most in the case of "***secondary dominants***," and other "*secondary chords*."

Secondary Dominants

What: Dominant seventh chords live, first and foremost, to resolve by perfect interval (down a perfect fifth or up a perfect fourth—counter-clockwise on the Circle) to their respective tonics, right? When a dominant seventh chord is built on a note *other than V*, and still resolves in this manner, it is acting as a dominant to a chord (or key) other than the tonic. It is then a *secondary dominant.*

Let's take a gander (or a goose) at a chord progression in the key of C. 𝄞

‖: C C^7 | F Dm | Em^7 A^7 | Dm^7 G^7 :‖

Up 'til now, we would have analyzed this progression like this:

‖: I I^7 | IV iim | $iiim^7$ VI^7 | iim^7 V^7 :‖

Here is the analysis of this progression taking into account secondary dominants.[17]

‖: I V^7/IV | IV iim | $iiim^7$ V^7/iim | iim^7 V^7 :‖

This time, the C^7 is called "five$^{(7)}$ of four" and the A^7 is called "five$^{(7)}$ of two."

Why call the chords by these obviously more complicated names? Here's why. The first analysis serves just fine to show where the chords fall *in the key*, but does not address how all of them *function in the context of this progression.* The second analysis is actually more descriptive of *what our ears hear.* The secondary dominants C^7 and A^7 "pulls us by the ears" to the chords that follow them. C^7 is the dominant seventh of the F chord, and A^7 is the dominant of the D (minor in this case) chord.

17 V/IV means "five of four," that is, the five chord of the four chord. The slash (/) means "of." In the key of C, a C7 generally functions as a secondary dominant of an F chord, or V7/IV. V7/iim means "the dominant seventh chord built on the fifth degree of the key of two." What a mouthful! Understanding the concept allows you to save some breath, and say, "five-seven of two," which, in the key of C would be A7, since two is Dm.

All of this put together is yet another example of the importance of the dominant-tonic relationship in music. Its importance is significant enough that we name a chord as a *secondary dominant* (V^7/IV, or V^7/iim for example) whenever possible, rather than as an *altered diatonic chord* (I^7 or VI^7).

In other words, in the key of F, C^7 is the V^7 chord. That means that C^7 just *loves* to pull to an F chord. This holds true even when we're *not* in the key of F. The example above is in C. An F chord is *IV* in the key of C. Therefore, C^7 to F is V^7/IV to *IV*.

The A^7 chord works similarly. A^7 is the V^7 chord in the key of D. Dm is the *iim* chord in the key of C. Therefore, in the above example, A^7 is V^7/iim (five^7 of two).

Secondary dominants can also simply be *major triads*, rather than sevenths. In C, a D triad usually acts as a secondary dominant of G (*V/V*), an E triad functions as a secondary dominant of Am (*V/vim*), and an A triad functions as five of Dm (*V/iim*).

Other Secondary Chords

As I said in chapter 14, dominants (*V* and V^7) are often preceded by accompanying subdominants (*IV*), and in jazz, supertonics (iim^7). The same goes for secondary dominants. Secondary dominants (*V/V* or V^7/V, for example) are often preceded by accompanying secondary subdominants (*IV/V* for example), or, especially in jazz, secondary supertonics (iim^7/V for example).

Any **nondiatonic** dominant seventh or major chord should be suspected as guilty of being a **secondary dominant** until proven innocent.

There is an occurrence of this in the previous chord progression. The Em^7 begins the motion that picks up momentum through the A^7 and arrives, seemingly inevitably, upon the Dm. The Em^7 is therefore *functioning* as iim^7/iim, or "two of two." I've mentioned that iim^7, V^7, *I* is a common diatonic progression. In some styles of music, most notably, jazz, it is *just as common* a secondary (***modulating***) progression. In other words, in the key of D, an Em^7 is the diatonic seventh chord built on the second degree of the scale. Since our progression is in the key of C, D is the second degree of the scale (*iim*). Therefore, Em^7 is, again, "two of two." Note that this is true even though the D chord is minor, rather than major.

The A^7, being a nondiatonic dominant seventh chord, has no other function in the key of C other than to pull to its temporary tonic of D minor—or major. So, until proven otherwise, we can, and should, assume that this will be its role.

So here is the latest, greatest analysis of the progression taking into account this "two-five of two" (in **bold**). (The Em^7 to A^7 is written "*$iim^7 – V^7/iim$*." This means "*iim^7/iim* to *V^7/iim*." The dash binds together the two secondary chords reflecting visually the relationship that exists musically.) 𝄞

‖: C C^7 | F Dm | **Em^7 A^7** | Dm^7 G^7 :‖

‖: I V^7/IV | IV iim | **iim^7– V^7/iim** | iim^7 V^7 :‖

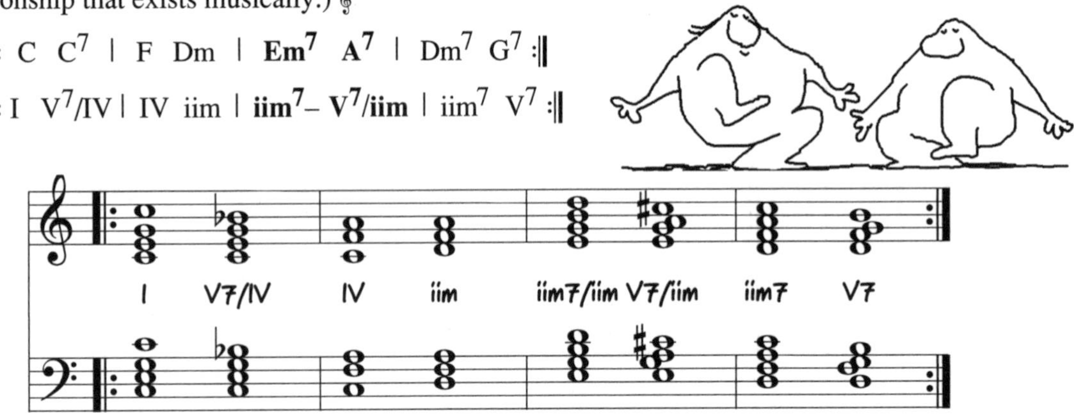

Progression Analyzed Using Secondary Chords

Multiple Secondary Dominants

Secondary dominants also just *love* to ride piggy-back. It is common in many styles of music to see as many as two to five secondary dominants in a row, setting up motion towards a seemingly inevitable last chord. For example, again in the key of C, an E may resolve to an A, which resolves to a D, which resolves to a G, which finally resolves to a C. I hate to say it, but that would make the E chord's function "*V/V/V/V*," or, in English, "five of five of five of five." Whew! Again, the words are unwieldy, *but* they are accurate in describing the chords' functions.

These chords could also be dominant sevenths:
C, E^7, A^7, D^7, G^7, C. 𝄞

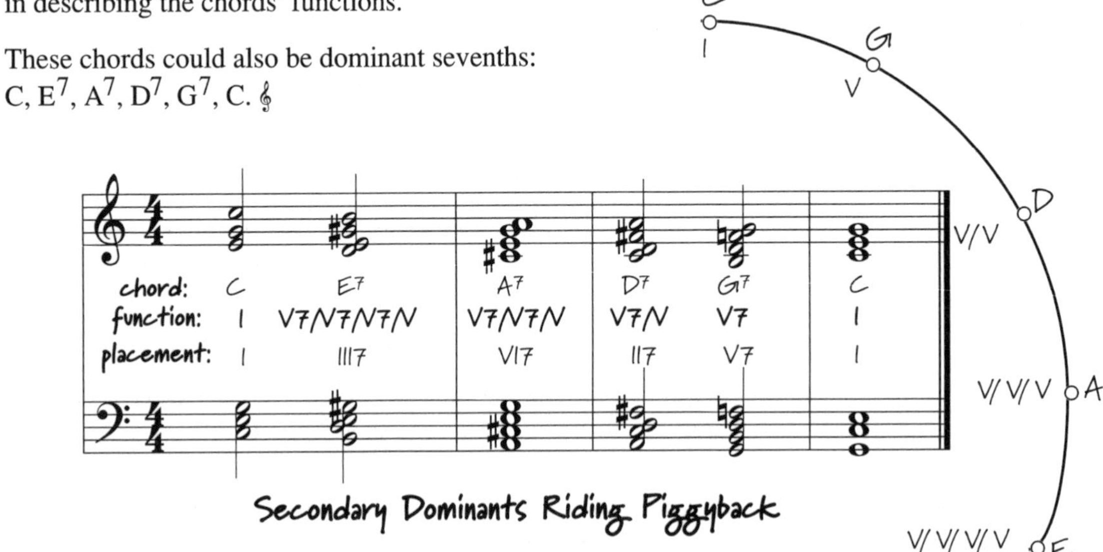

Secondary Dominants Riding Piggyback

This is Circle of Fifths stuff, gang! Did you realize? Take a look at this ↗ Circle fragment.

Especially in jazz, this is often taken further, with a number of ***modulating*** (changing key) two-fives in a row. Often, the temporary tonic of the two-five appears, in turn becoming a secondary two itself. (Notice that this situation makes for two-fives descending in whole-steps, and that the resolution of the G chord to the C is delayed—interrupted by the Gm chord.) This example is in the key of F.

Am^7 D^7	G	Gm^7 C^7	F^6	‖
iim^7–V^7/V/V	V/V	iim^7 V^7	I^6	‖ …or…
iim^7–V^7/II	V/V	iim^7 V^7	I^6	‖

Other times, the temporary tonic is also *simultaneously* a secondary two:

Am^7 D^7	Gm^7 C^7	Fm^7 B♭^{7}	E♭$^{6/9}$	‖
iim^7–V^7/iim/iim	iim^7/iim V^7/iim	iim^7 V^7	I$^{6/9}$	‖

Often, the temporary tonic doesn't even appear, as in the following common progression. This is an instance of *deceptive resolution*, i.e., when the chord does not resolve in the way we expect. (Notice that, in this case, the two-fives ascend by whole-steps.)

Am^7 D^7	Bm^7 E^7	C#m^7 F#^{7}	BM^7	‖
iim^7–V^7/♭VI	iim^7–V^7/♭VII	iim^7 V^7	IM^7	‖

"Sweet Georgia Brown" is a great example of piggy-backed secondary dominants. Here are the chords to the song in the key of F:

D^7		G^7		|
C^7		F / C^7 /	F	|
D^7		G^7		|
Dm / A^7 /	Dm / A^7 /	F / D^7 /	G^7 C^7 F /	‖

Analyzing the song's chord progression in terms of chord *function* makes these "piggy-backs" very easy to find:

V^7/V^7/V^7		V^7/V^7		|
V^7		I / V^7 /	I	|
V^7/V^7/V^7		V^7/V^7		|
vim / V^7/vim /	vim / V^7/vim /	I / V^7/V^7/V^7 /	V^7/V^7 V^7 I /	‖

On the other hand, analyzing the song in terms of chord *location*, while *much* easier to read and find the chords on the fly, very much obscures the secondary dominants:

VI^7		II^7		|
V^7		I / V^7 /	I	|
VI^7		II^7		|
vim / III^7 /	vim / III^7 /	I / VI^7 /	II^7 V^7 I /	‖

This brings you to a choice: which way to analyze progressions like this in your own work. I don't believe that one method is right and one is wrong. Which to choose depends on your goal—your reason for doing the analysis, or for writing the chords in terms of how they fall in the key. If you want to show how the chords are really interacting, the first method is the one for you. If you want the chords to be read quickly and easily, the second method is probably the better choice.

Numerous examples of all of these and more can be found in any jazz standards "fake book." Ask at your local music store.

Changing a secondary dominant to a minor triad or minor seventh chord strips it of its secondary dominant status. It would then not be functioning as a secondary dominant. It can, and very often does, still participate in the circle of fifths momentum—often as a *secondary two* (iim^7/?) instead of as a secondary dominant (V^7/?).

Here is an illustration of this, using the progression from the beginning of this section:

1. | C / E^7 / | A^7 | D^7 / G^7 / | C ‖ Watch:

2. | C / Em^7 / | Am^7 | D^7 / G^7 / | C ‖ Or even:

3. | C / Em^7 / | Am^7 | Dm^7 / G^7 / | C ‖

Look, ma, no more secondary dominants! All gone. But the roots are still moving by perfect intervals, so we still have a chord progression based on the circle of fifths.

Having just stripped a chord progression of all its secondary dominants, let's reverse the process, and give our pal Susannah a pair of secondary dominants: the two Dm^7 chords now become D^7s. Notice how much more the D^7 pulls to the G^7 than did the Dm^7.

F **Dm^7** **Em^7** **Am** **D^7** **G^7** **Em^7** **Am** **D^7** **G^7** **C**
Oh, Susannah, don't you cry for me, for I come from Alabama with my banjo on my knee.

IV **iim^7** **$iiim^7$** **vim** **V^7/V** **V^7** **$iiim^7$** **vim** **V^7/V** **V^7** **I**
Oh, Susannah, don't you cry for me, for I come from Alabama with my banjo on my knee.

Oh Susannah: With Two Secondary Dominants

...better play the bass clef line up an octave to avoid the dreaded "mud in ear" syndrome.

Let's take Susannah a step further by changing most of the other minor (seventh) chords into secondary dominants. Then we'll have a discussion about whether this *works* in the context of this song.

In the following example, "V^7/…" means "five^7 of the following chord." This saves space (especially as an alternative to "V^7/V/V/V/V" in the case of the B^7). 𝄞

F **B^7** **E^7** **A^7** **D^7** **G^7** **E^7** **A^7** **D^7** **G^7** **C**
Oh, Susannah, don't you cry for me, for I come from Alabama with my banjo on my knee.

IV **V^7/…** **V^7/…** **V^7/…V^7…** **V^7** **V^7/V/V/V** **V^7/V/V** **V^7/V** **V^7** **I**
Oh, Susannah, don't you cry for me, for I come from Alabama with my banjo on my knee.

"Oh Susannah" With as Many Secondary Dominants as Possible

It's discussion time! Play this alone or with a friend. What do you think of the sound of these new seventh chords in the context of this song? Are they successful, or do they detract from the overall effect?

Personally, I would throw every one of these out, and revert to the previous version, or look elsewhere for harmonic fulfillment. The B^7 is just a *bit* "too much." (Changing the B note to a C, though, would give us an F#$^{\circ 7}$ chord, which would work just fine. In fact, this is a common approach to this progression and others like it.) The G notes in the melody against the G# notes in the E^7 chord conflict with each other, as do the melody's C♮ against the C# of the A^7 chord. So, unless you want a high degree of tension, then I would say these chords are too forced, and do not particularly work. With the exception of the F#$^{\circ 7}$ that I mentioned, I'd say that the previous version worked much better.

Finally, let's revisit chapter 14 and have a closer look at one particular chord's function in a minor key: the *♭VII* chord. You guessed it: in minor keys, *♭VII* often acts as a secondary dominant (*V/♭III*). This *secondary dominant function* is perhaps this chord's most important role in minor keys.

Modulating with Secondary Chords

Secondary dominants and friends are often used to ***modulate***, or *change key*. Changing key gives a song or piece a fresh sound. Pop composers love to modulate up a half-step or whole-step, or even a minor or major third. Since none of these keys are within one notch on the Circle, they are not very closely related, and the key change comes as a nice kick. Let's enlist Susannah to help out with this one. She has been in the key of C all along, but now uses an A♭^{7} as a ***pivot chord***[18], to modulate into the key of D♭, where the song could continue. 𝄞

Em^7 Am^7 D^7 G^7 C A♭^{7} D♭...
...for I come from Alabama with my banjo on my knee. (now in key of D♭)

iiim^7 vim^7 V^7/V V^7 I V^7/... I
...for I come from Alabama with my banjo on my knee. (new key a half-step higher)

In the Roman numeral analysis above, the warning (new key a half-step higher) is necessary to make it clear that the final *I* chord is actually a *half-step higher* than the preceding *I* chord. Different people handle this differently. Some people always write the key at the beginning in a square above the Roman numerals. A *relative* explanation such as (new key: a fifth lower), or whatever, is also fine, especially if you don't particularly want to plop the progression into any particular key.

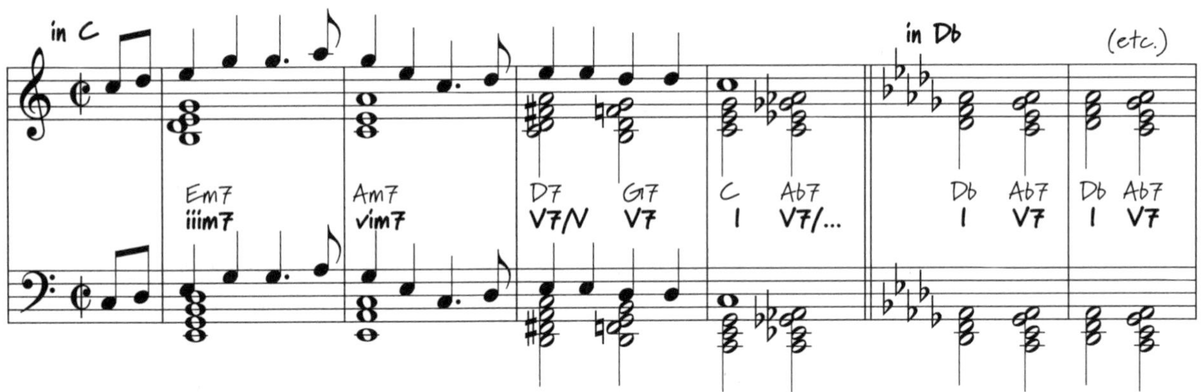

Using a Secondary Dominant to Modulate Into a New Key

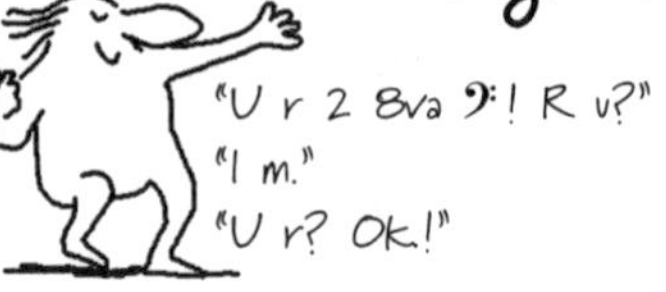

18 A **pivot chord** is a chord which acts as a doorway, or pivot, into a new key, as in the case of the first Ab7 chord in the Susannah example above.

Chapter 18~ Transposition

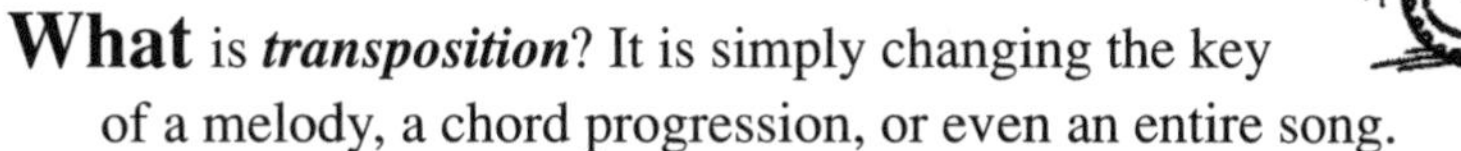

What is ***transposition***? It is simply changing the key of a melody, a chord progression, or even an entire song.

Why might one want to transpose? Common reasons include: to put a song within a certain singer's vocal range, or a certain instrument's best playing range, or to allow instrumentalists to play in a key with fewer accidentals, or for a *transposing instrument* to read from *concert key* sheet music (all explained below… don't worry!). Lastly, transposition is used part way through a song in the form of *modulation* (changing key), to "freshen" the aural palette, and especially in pop music, to create a feeling of increased intensity, as I explained on the previous page.

Basic Transposition… Transposing Melodies

How does one transpose? The most basic way to transpose a melody is to use the chromatic scale, and move each note the same number of half-steps up or down. A common example of this is men and women singing the same melody together. Women's vocal ranges are naturally about an octave higher than those of men. Singing the same melody separated by an octave is the simplest transposition: *octave transposition.*

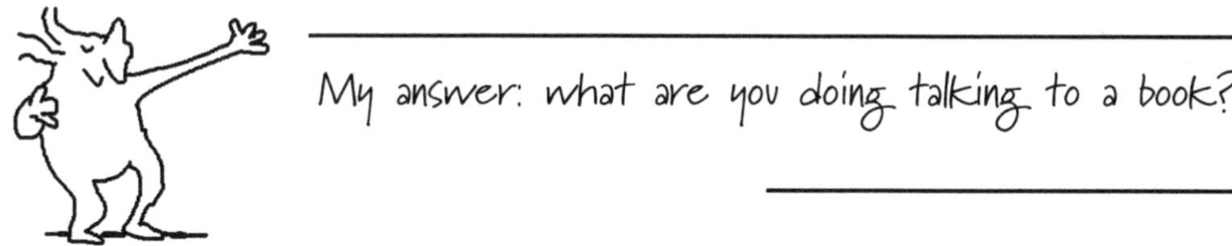

Some melodies fall into a range that men and women share. In this case, they can sing in unison. An example requiring a bit more thought on the part of the transposer is a melody which is a bit too low for the female singer and a bit too high for the male singer to sing in unison. A solution for this is to transpose the melody up, for example, five half-steps for the woman, and down seven half-steps for the man.

One *could* use this method (of transposing using half-steps) to transpose any distance, but there is an easier way for anyone comfortable with intervals. This easier, quicker, way is to transpose *by interval.* If you know your intervals, transposing each chord or melody note in the previous examples up or down the appropriate interval is a breeze. Up five half-steps is a perfect fourth, and down seven half-steps is a perfect fifth. Why count half-steps when you can calculate by interval? So, both of these techniques yield the same result: the men and women will be singing in octaves in the key a fourth higher (or a fifth lower).

More Advanced Transposition... Transposing Chords

Chords can also be transposed. I'll show you an example, but one last thing first...and then, the next thing... before anything else. I promise. Here it is: when transposing chords, change only *the root of the chord!* Do *not* change the suffix (chord type) at all. (If this isn't clear to you, I'd suggest you review "Overview of Basic Chord Anatomy" in chapter 5.) *This is important!* If you were to change the *chord type,* you'd be *reharmonizing* (changing the harmony), not transposing.

For example, take the chord progression Em, E♭, A♭maj^7, G^6, and transpose the roots up a minor third. Don't touch those suffixes! You wind up with Gm, F#, Bmaj^7 B♭^{6}. Easy!

Using either of the two previous methods (transposing everything by moving the roots a number of half-steps or by an interval), you don't even have to know what key the original chord progression or melody is in (perish the thought). This could be helpful, for example, if the original key is ambiguous.

If the key is clear, or you're willing to assume a certain key, then there is a better way to transpose. This method requires more knowledge, but if you've digested keys and such, then you're ready. You must first understand how the chords fit in the original key. Then you merely reproduce those relationships in the new key. This method more accurately describes what is going on in the music. Rather than "transposing blindly" anything that is dished out, you call upon your knowledge of keys, diatonic chords, diatonic chord functions, and nondiatonic chords, and merely reproduce in the key of your choice what is going on in the original key. This is more difficult at first, but in the end is faster, more reliable, and probably easier.

Our previous example of Em, E♭, A♭maj^7, G^6 is probably in the key of G. The context would help decide, but for our purposes, G will work just fine. In G, this progression would be: *vim, ♭VI, ♭IImaj*^{7}*, I*^{6}.

Using these numbers, the chords can easily be transposed into any key—as long as you know the major scale for that key.

1. An F major scale is F, G, A, B♭, C, D, E, F.
2. In F, *vim* is Dm, ♭*VI* is D♭, ♭*II*maj^7 is G♭maj^7, and *I*^{6} is F^6.
3. Therefore, in F, the progression would be Dm, D♭, G♭maj^7, F^6.

If you saw the original progression as being in a different key, the numbers would be different, but the relationships of the chords to each other would be identical. Watch.

If you assumed this progression to be in the key of C, you would have analyzed it as follows: *iiim, ♭III, ♭VImaj*^{7}*, V*^{6}.

Using this new perspective, let's transpose this progression into the key of B♭.

1. The B♭ major scale is B♭, C, D, E♭, F, G, A, B♭.
2. In the key of B♭, *iiim* is Dm, ♭*III* is D♭, ♭*VI*maj^7 is G♭maj^7, and *V*^{6} is F^6.
3. So, in B♭, the progression would be Dm, D♭, G♭maj^7, F^6.

Eureka!! It's the same result either way!

Now, I'll admit, I set this up so you would see that this method works even if you don't *really* know the key. Even with ambiguous progressions, if you do your math right, you get the right result. Of course, in real world examples (such as songs… remember them?), the key is clear, as long as you know your key signatures, so this is not an issue.

The quickest way to transpose is based on the preceding method, but is one step more advanced. It involves understanding keys well enough that you can think of (and ideally, *hear*) what you're playing, whether melodies or chords, in *non-key-specific* terms. This would mean that you are sufficiently aware of the chords' (or notes') relationships to each other, that you see (and hear) the original key as just *one of twelve possibilities*. That is, instead of thinking of C, F, and G^7, you think of *I*, *IV*, and V^7 occurring, *in this case*, in the key of C. Again, if you know your keys and scales well enough, it is easy to think of *I*, *IV*, and V^7 in any of the twelve keys. You can be thinking in all keys at once, or no key at all, depending on whether your personal musical cup is half full or half empty.

You can be thinking in all keys at once, or no key at all, depending on whether your personal musical cup is half full or half empty.

Transposing, like many other things new and unfamiliar, feels difficult and very intellectual at first. The more you do it, though, the more it will come naturally, and be something you do by feel rather than by brute thought. Stick with it. Whether it takes you days or months, you will see what I mean. With persistence, you'll be able to transpose easily. If it is any consolation, know that you will be alive and well and playing for years to come—whether or not you take it upon yourself to learn transposition, any of the concepts in this book, unicycle riding, juggling, or gardening. The choice is whether or not you will be a playing, transposing, unicycle riding juggling gardener… or not. Sorry to preach. Go for it.

Transposition and "Transposing Instruments"

What: Another real world use of transposition has to do with reading music and the fact that some instruments are *transposing* rather than ***concert pitch*** instruments. You see, when a piano or a flute reads a note from sheet music, that actual note comes out of the instrument. On the other hand, when a trumpet, soprano sax, or clarinet reads a note from sheet music, the note that comes out is a whole-step *lower* than the note they "think" they are playing. Specifically, these three are B♭ instruments. The alto and baritone sax are E♭ instruments, or are "in E♭," and the French horn is in F. There are other transposing instruments too, but you get the point.

How do you figure out what note will come out when an instrument plays a note that its player thinks is a C… but isn't? Here's the formula for transposing instruments: for an instrument in the key of X, X is the note that sounds when the instrument plays "its" C. For example, when an alto sax plays the fingering for a C note, the listener hears an E♭, so the alto sax is in E♭. When the clarinet plays the note that its player thinks of as C, the note heard is a B♭.

By the way, some C instruments also transpose… but at the interval of one or more octaves.

One instance where transposition is important is when a transposing instrument has to read from sheet music intended for a non transposing instrument, or vice versa.

Here's a chart of some common transposing instruments. The first column has the instrument's name and key. The second column has the note that will come out when the instrument plays its C. The third column lists what a player would have to do to make the note *sound as written.*

Key/Instrument	Sounds	To Sound as Written, play…
C piccolo	C (one octave higher)	an octave lower
B♭ clarinet	B♭ (whole-step lower)	a whole-step higher
B♭ trumpet	B♭ (whole-step lower)	a whole-step higher
E♭ alto sax	E♭ (major sixth lower)	a major sixth higher
B♭ tenor sax	B♭ (major ninth lower)	a major ninth (or whole-step) higher
French horn in F	F (perfect fifth lower)	a perfect fifth higher
bass	C (octave lower)	an octave higher
guitar	C (octave lower)	an octave higher

Why: You say, "That seems like a complicated way of doing things! Why don't all instruments sound at concert pitch?" My answer is, "What are you doing talking to a book? Do you do this often?" Seriously, the answer is that musical instruments evolved from relatively simple and limited origins into the relatively sophisticated instruments of today. Back before wind instruments had valves and (finger) keys, certain (musical) keys were very difficult—if not impossible, depending on the instrument—to finger smoothly. One solution was to have available several sizes of the same instrument, in different keys. As valves and keys became standard, certain sizes of the instrument were more popular with composers and players, and you guessed it, those weren't necessarily always the ones at concert pitch. Hence, our current day hodgepodge of mixed-key instruments.

One instance where transposition becomes important is when a transposing instrument has to read from sheet music intended for a non transposing instrument, or vice versa. In either case, if the player were to read the music without transposing, the sound would be very different from what the composer or arranger intended! Sight transposition is something that can, in time, be developed such that a transposing reader can read at a respectable rate, right along with a non transposing one. All of the above transposition techniques are also available to a sight-transposer.

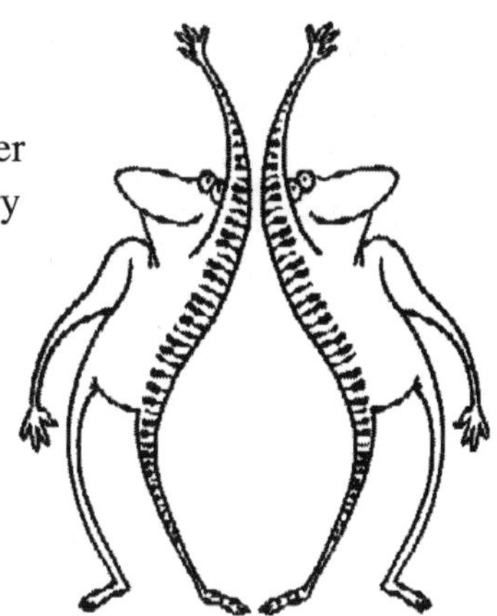

Transposing by Changing Clefs

Here's yet another chance for me to plug musical literacy: reading in treble, bass, alto, and tenor clefs can be immensely helpful in the situations we're discussing, as well as for reading (and writing) scores in any style… end of sermon. Here's how it might work for three of the most common transpositions: When playing a B♭ instrument, but reading a part written at concert pitch (non transposing) in treble clef, read one octave higher in alto clef, changing the key signature to that of the key a whole step higher.

Conversely, when playing a concert pitch instrument, but reading a part written in B♭, treble clef, read one octave higher in tenor clef, in the key a whole step lower. When reading a part written in treble clef in E♭ on a concert instrument, read in bass clef an octave higher, in the key a minor third higher.

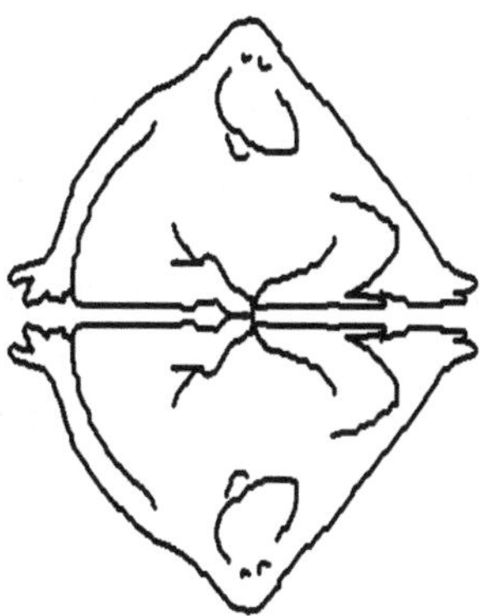

For other transpositions, I find the other techniques easier than this clef/key changing technique. Experiment and see what works for you. You may find, after some experience, that you become fluid enough with the various transposing techniques that you can go back and forth between several methods, even in the course of the same piece! Now go make some great music!

Chapter 19~ Cadences

What/When: ***Cadences*** occur at the end of a phrase, or the end of *part* of a phrase. A cadence consists of two or more chords that interrupt the harmonic momentum. The interruption can be temporary, in the form of arriving at a point of tension, or arriving at resolution. Analogies in language include phrases ending with a comma or question mark in the case of tension, or with a period in the case of resolution.

Why: The saying goes, "all good things must come to an end." This is equally true for music. If you can recognize the most common ways in which phrases end, you are that much farther ahead in understanding all musical phrasing.

Cadences in "Oh Susannah" fall on the words "me" (tension), and "on my knee" (resolution):

"Oh, Susannah, don't you cry for **me**, cause I come from Alabama with my banjo **on my knee**."

Susannah appears yet again in even brighter colors in order for us to look at the most important cadence types: full, half, plagal, and deceptive. 𝄞 (Each cadence is enclosed in parentheses in the example below.) In the last cadence (plagal), she even goes to church! But first, let me mention **why** you might want to learn about cadences. If you can recognize and identify cadences, you will be able to recognize melodic and harmonic patterns much more easily, and understand better how music is put together. Enticed? I hope so.

Cadences in "Oh Susannah"

Cadence Types & Definitions

The **full cadence** is **V**$^{(7)}$ —▷ **I** and again corresponds with moving from *tension*, and arriving at *resolution*. In written language, this corresponds to a phrase ending in a period or exclamation point. Technically, a cadence is only "full" if the tonic is in both the melody and bass. 𝄞

The **half cadence** is **something** —▷ **V**$^{(7)}$, that is, just about *any* chord moving to the dominant. In language, a half cadence corresponds to a phrase ending in a comma or question mark. A half cadence creates the expectation that something will indeed come next because of the unresolved nature of the dominant. The listener knows that the song or piece is not over at this point, unless the composer or player is being cheeky, or *deceptive* (see below). The chord preceding the dominant chord is often *its own dominant,* or the *V/V* ("five of five," as it's called). In the same way that the dominant pulls to the tonic, the secondary dominant pulls to the dominant, creating the effect of a "temporary tonic." How temporary this ends up being depends totally on the situation, and can be anywhere from a beat or two to a whole section of a piece. 𝄞

The **plagal cadence** is **IV** —▷ **I**. You've heard it in the amens sung and played in church. It shows up elsewhere, too, but usually to invoke that "churchy sound." 𝄞

A **deceptive cadence** is simply any cadence that doesn't do what you expect it to. More specifically, a deceptive cadence is usually **V**$^{(7)}$ (since the dominant creates such a high level of expectation) to something other than **I**. The deceptive cadences found in classical, jazz, and pop musics differ in destination chords, but the effect is similar in each case… one of foiled expectation. The **mediant** and **submediant** chords are the most standard tonic substitutes—the submediant (*vim*), in the case of classical music, and the mediant (*iiim*), in the case of jazz. (Notice that each of these two triads shares two of its three notes with the tonic triad! This might help you see how they might easily get away with replacing the tonic.) 𝄞

Most common **deceptive cadences**:

V$^{(7)}$ —> **vim** (classical and pop)
V$^{(7)}$ —> **iiim** (jazz and pop)
V$^{(7)}$ —> **im** (when key is major)
V$^{(7)}$ —> **I** (when key is minor)
V$^{(7)}$—> **IV** (gospel, pop, etc.)
V$^{(7)}$ —> ♭**VI** (various pop, classical, etc)

Chapter 20~
Tritone Substitution

Who: This chapter is an *absolute must* for all you jazzers! The rest of you might find it interesting, too. It turns out that the ***tritone***, maligned and ostracized for years, is vital to certain jazz chord progressions. Whether you've known it or not, if you've listened to much jazz at all, you've heard the substitute V^7 chord exert its strong magnetic pull. Stay tuned for the steamy story of ***tritone substitution*** and the ***subV***^{7} chord…

What: The *subV*^{7} chord is a dominant seventh chord that can substitute for ("sub" is short for "substitute"), or follow, the V^7 chord. The *subV*^{7} chord is built on the note a tritone away from the dominant, on the lowered second degree (♭2) of the key. It looks like, and in fact *is,* a ♭II^7. In the key of C, *subV*^{7} is D♭^{7}, while V^7 is, as you know, G^7. 𝄞

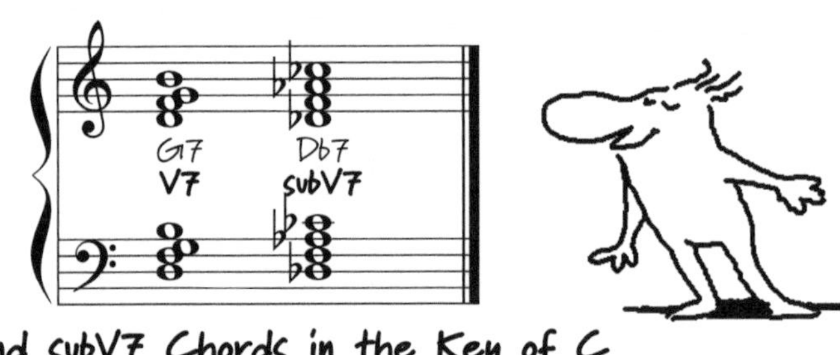

V7 and subV7 Chords in the Key of C

How does it work?

1. Besides other intervals of varying interest, dominant seventh chords contain a tritone—from the third to the seventh. For example, a D7 chord (D, F♯, A, C) contains the tritone F♯ to C. 𝄞

2. The notes of that tritone are shared by **two** dominant seventh chords. They are D^7 and… you tell me. This is because the interval of a tritone inverts to a tritone (see chapter 8). So, the tritone from the D7 chord inverts to the tritone C to F♯. If you respell this "C to G♭," and ask, "of what root are these the third and flat seventh," the answer "A♭" will leap into your head—I hope. 𝄞 Indeed, A♭^{7} *is* the other dominant seventh chord containing this tritone.

3. The two previously mentioned dominant seventh chords are built on roots separated by a—you guessed it—tritone: D and A♭. 𝄞

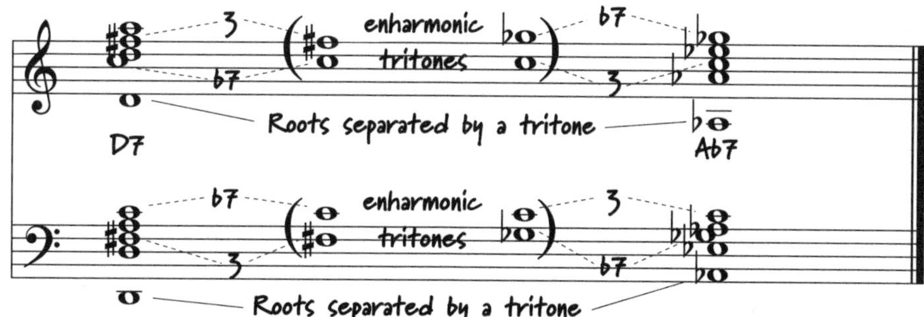

Shared Tritones in Dominant Seventh Chords Built a Tritone Apart

"So what," you may say. Ah. It turns out that this shard tritone makes the two chords interchangeable in many jazz situations. You were introduced to diatonic chord substitution back in chapter 10. This is an example of *chromatic substitution.*

In jazz, the *subV*^{7} is often substituted for the *V*^{7} chord. 𝄞 The sub five can also *follow* the five chord instead of replacing it. 𝄞

original:	$\mid$ V^7	$\mid$ I	‖
substituting:	$\mid$ subV^7	$\mid$ I	‖
following:	$\mid$ V^7 subV^7	$\mid$ I	‖

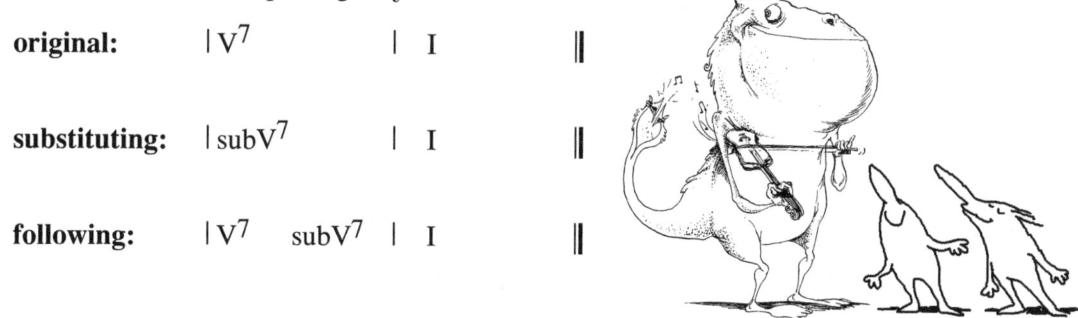

original progression — Dm7 iim7, G7 V7, Cmaj7 Imaj7
subV7 substituting for V7 — Dm7 iim7, D♭7 subV7, Cmaj7 Imaj7
subV7 following V7 — Dm7 iim7, G7 V, D♭7 subV7, Cmaj7 Imaj7

Treating a iim7, V7, Imaj7 Progression to SubV7s

One of the things that makes jazz sound like jazz is the prevalence of chords larger than sevenths (ninths, elevenths, and thirteenths, coming up soon), and chromatically altered chords (m$^{7\flat5}$, $^{7\sharp9}$, etc.). The above progressions will sound even more authentic if you come back to them after learning the higher extensions.

The "Substitute iim7" chord

We've talked about the importance in jazz of the *iim*^{7}, *V*^{7} progression and the *subV*^{7} chord. It turns out that the minor seventh chord built a tritone away from the *iim*^{7} chord (♭*vim*^{7}, or even "*sub iim*^{7}," although you don't hear this name as much in polite conversation) is also an important player. This chord can be found preceding both the *V*^{7} chord *and* the *subV*^{7} chord. Here are some examples using these substitute chords: 𝄞

| iim^7 V^7 | Imaj^7 ||

| iim^7 subV^7 | Imaj^7 ||

| subiim^7 subV^7 | Imaj^7 ||

| subiim^7 V^7 | Imaj^7 ||

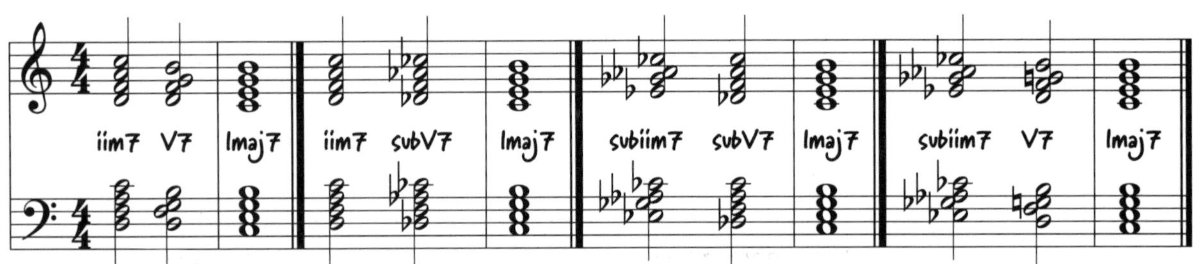

Examples of SubV7 and Subiim7

Examples of these progressions can be found already built into songs on almost any page of any fake book[19], or jazz sheet music. See if you can find some. Start by looking at songs such as *Satin Doll, Girl from Ipanema,* and *How High the Moon*, and certainly don't stop there!

19 A fake book has songs with just the melody, chord symbols, and perhaps a sketchy suggestion as to style. The musician is expected to "fake" the accompaniment. There are advantages and disadvantages to this approach. The disadvantages have to do with the fact that a **lot** is left up to the musician reading the music. An advantage is the reader is not laden with extraneous information: someone else's arrangement of the piece. The creativity is left to you. The more you know what you are doing, the more you can do with the material. Another advantage is that much more music can fit into a smaller space, so you get a lot more songs for your money.

Chapter 21~ Natural Modes

The Importance of Modes: Another Pep Talk

What: ***Modes*** are yet another type of scale. The ***natural modes*** come directly from the major scale and can be approached and conceived of in two different ways, explained below in the **How** section. Record any of your favorite TV shows, relax, and read on.

Why learn about modes? Modes are useful for a number of reasons. First, a lot of folk music from all around the world is ***modal*** (using modes), rather than ***tonal*** (using major/minor scales or keys). Second, modes are very useful for improvisation in various styles. Third, the "one dozen eggs versus twelve eggs" analogy holds true for modes just as it does for major scales: modes exist whether you understand them or not; why not package them? Being able to think modally will make you a better musician!

How: *The first way* to derive modes is merely to choose a scale and "reassign" the role of *tonic* to each of the other notes in the scale while keeping all the original notes of the scale unchanged. Each "reassignment" yields a different mode. The first mode is the major scale itself (Ionian is its modal name: 1-1; C, D, E, F, G, A, B, C). Starting the scale from the second degree and going up to the second degree an octave higher will give you the second mode (Dorian: 2-2; D, E, F, G, A, B, C, D). Reassigning the title and role of "tonic" to the third degree and going to the third degree an octave higher gives you the third mode (Phrygian: 3-3; E, F, G, A, B, C, D, E), and so on. Using this method, you define each mode by *the degree of the major scale on which it starts.*

With this method, you end up with each mode beginning on a *different note* of a major scale. This works well as an initial way to derive the modes. Once you've done this, however, there is a second way to think of *the very same* modes which ends up being more practical in everyday musical applications.

That *second way* is to define each mode by how it differs from a major scale beginning on the *same tonic*. How would we alter a D major scale (D, E, F#, G, A, B, C#, D) to get D Dorian mode (D, E, F, G, A, B, C, D)? How would we need to alter an E major scale (E, F#, G#, A, B, C#, D#, E) to get E Phrygian mode (E, F, G, A, B, C, D, E)? Did we lower the seventh degree (note) a half-step? Did we lower the third and seventh degrees a half-step? This is similar to how we defined minor scales earlier.

Using this second method, we think of modes as chromatically altered major scales. As I said, this generally ends up being more useful in real life.

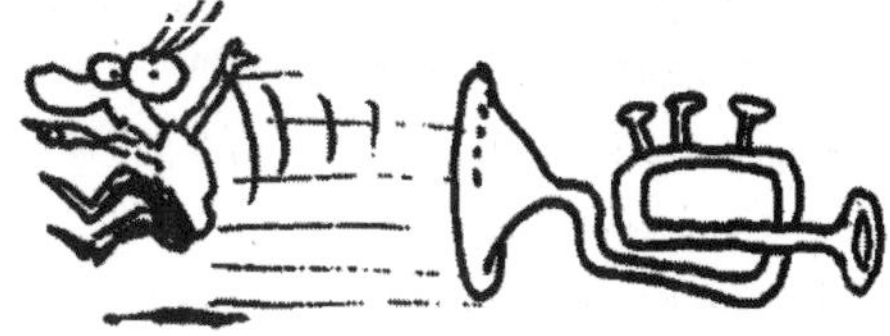

What we'll do here is use the first method (the "move the tonic" method) to initially figure out the mode, and then contrast the resulting mode with the major scale beginning on the *same tonic* as the mode's tonic. This will result in looking at the mode according to the second method, the "keep the tonic the same and alter the scale degrees" method.

First, I'll walk you through the general process of deriving a mode. Then I'll show you a specific example, and then … you're on your own. First, write out two octaves or so of your current favorite major scale. Number each scale degree using the numbers 1–7, since 8 and 1 are the same note on different octaves. Then reassign the title of *tonic* to a different note in the scale. Finally, compare your newfound mode with the major scale beginning on the *same tonic* as the mode. How do they differ? What notes in the major scale are raised or lowered for it to become that mode? The altered notes are one way of defining the mode.

Let's use Dorian mode, which begins on the second degree of the major scale. Skip the initial major scale tonic, and look at the notes from 2 to 2. Now compare your newfound Dorian mode with the major scale beginning on *the same tonic as the mode*. How do they differ? What notes of the Dorian are raised or lowered in comparison to the major scale? Find these, and you have defined the Dorian mode.

I'll do one to get you started. Any key would work. I'll use F major for our sample. Here is over an octave of an F major scale. The notes from 2 to 2 are in **bold.** 𝄞

1 **2 3 4 5 6 7 1 2** 3 4 5 …

F **G A B♭ C D E F G** A B♭ C …

Now let's extract the notes from G to G (or 2 to 2).

2 3 4 5 6 7 1 2

G A B♭ C D E F G

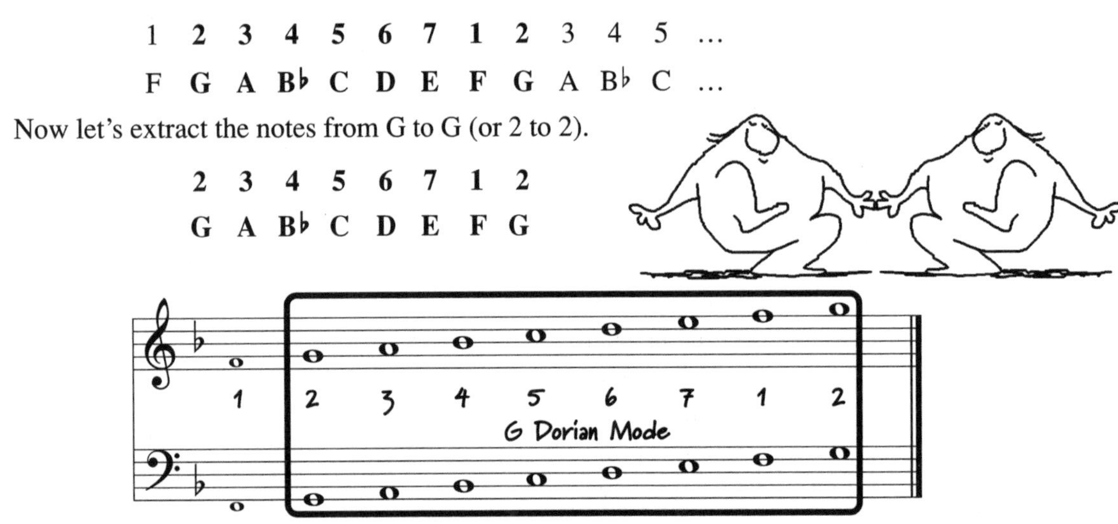

Deriving G Dorian From an F Major Scale: First Step (Numbers Not Adjusted)

… but again, we are left with a scale beginning and ending *on 2*! That's no way for a scale to live. Scales like to begin and end on 1, right? But if we merely renumber this Dorian mode 1–8, we have a different problem: 1–8 describes a major scale, which is different from Dorian mode. So we must show how G Dorian mode *differs* from the G major scale by showing chromatic alterations.

So we need to answer the question, "how did we alter the notes of the key of G major to arrive at G Dorian?" The answer is that we lowered the third and seventh, each by a half-step. So we can now safely define Dorian mode as a major scale with a ♭3, and a ♭7. 𝄞

Dorian:	1	2	♭3	4	5	6	♭7	(8)
G Dorian:	G	A	B♭	C	D	E	F	G
G major:	G	A	B	C	D	E	F♯	G
Major:	1	2	3	4	5	6	7	(8)

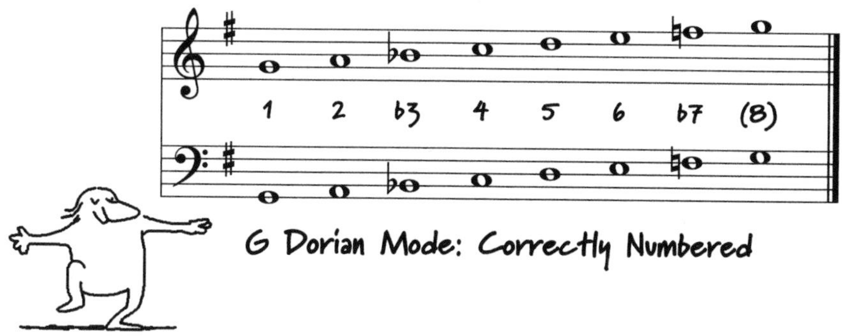

G Dorian Mode: Correctly Numbered

Yo!! When defining scales in this way, "♭" and "♯" refer to notes altered from the major scale, not absolute flats and sharps. Again, make sure you compare each scale degree with the same scale degree from the major scale beginning on the *same tonic.*

The "one dozen eggs versus twelve eggs" analogy holds true for modes just as it does for major scales: modes exist whether you understand them or not; why not package them?

When first learning about modes, it's very helpful to play a tonic drone (a repeated or sustained note) in the bass range as you play or sing the mode. This keeps your ear centered on the mode's tonic. Otherwise, it is likely that ears new to playing modes will hear a major scale "starting on the wrong note" rather than the mode from tonic to tonic.

Now it's your turn. Mode Worksheet Number One is incomplete. Your job is to complete it by filling in the chromatic alterations. Using an F major scale, apply the same process used above. Begin on successively higher scale degrees each time. Add a flat (to show a lowered scale tone) or a sharp (to show a raised scale tone) to the left of any altered scale degree number, as necessary. For those of you who prefer to work using standard notation, blank staff paper is provided on the next page. Answers appear in upcoming pages.

Stay tuned.

Mode Worksheet Number One

MODE NUMBER/NAME/COMPARE TO...	MODE DEGREES							
1. ***Ionian Mode*** (major scale)	1	2	3	4	5	6	7	(8)
F major (compare to F major)	F	G	A	B♭	C	D	E	(F)
2. ***Dorian Mode***	1	2	3	4	5	6	7	(8)
G Dorian (compare to G major)	G	A	B♭	C	D	E	F	(G)
3. ***Phrygian Mode***	1	2	3	4	5	6	7	(8)
A Phrygian (compare to A major)	A	B♭	C	D	E	F	G	(A)
4. ***Lydian Mode***	1	2	3	4	5	6	7	(8)
B♭ Lydian (compare to B♭ major)	B♭	C	D	E	F	G	A	(B♭)
5. ***Mixolydian Mode***	1	2	3	4	5	6	7	(8)
C Mixolydian (compare to C major)	C	D	E	F	G	A	B♭	(C)
6. ***Aeolian Mode*** (natural minor scale)	1	2	3	4	5	6	7	(8)
D Aeolian (compare to D major)	D	E	F	G	A	B♭	C	(D)
7. ***Locrian Mode***	1	2	3	4	5	6	7	(8)
E Locrian (compare to E major)	E	F	G	A	B♭	C	D	(E)

Lest you feel confused, all scales (and modes) begin on *their own tonic!* For example, G Dorian is a G major scale with a lowered third and seventh (and having the same notes as an F major scale—but beginning on G). F Phrygian is an F major scale with a ♭2, ♭3, ♭6, and ♭7, indeed beginning on F; and yes, having the same notes as a D♭ major scale.

Your Very Own Modal Workspace

Now let's get rid of any "key specific information." In other words, let's assemble a mode chart that applies to *all keys*. *This is another incomplete template*. Again, fill in the chromatic alterations. Also, at the far right, write the number of notes altered (raised or lowered) compared to the major scale beginning on the same note as each mode.

Mode Worksheet #2 A

MODE NUMBER AND NAME				MODE DEGREES					♭s/#s
1. Ionian (Major)	1	2	3	4	5	6	7	(8)	_____
2. Dorian	1	2	3	4	5	6	7	(8)	_____
3. Phrygian	1	2	3	4	5	6	7	(8)	_____
4. Lydian	1	2	3	4	5	6	7	(8)	_____
5. Mixolydian	1	2	3	4	5	6	7	(8)	_____
6. Aeolian (Natural Minor)	1	2	3	4	5	6	7	(8)	_____
7. Locrian	1	2	3	4	5	6	7	(8)	_____

Now circle the half-steps in each mode. Not surprisingly, you'll see a pattern.

In case you had trouble with the preceding exercises, here is a chart of the modes of C major, this time, to help you along.

Modes Chart 1

C	D	E	F	G	A	B	C							**C Ionian**
	D	E	F	G	A	B	C	D						**D Dorian**
		E	F	G	A	B	C	D	E					**E Phrygian**
F Lydian			F	G	A	B	C	D	E	F				
G Mixolydian				G	A	B	C	D	E	F	G			
A Aeolian					A	B	C	D	E	F	G	A		
B Locrian						B	C	D	E	F	G	A	B	

Modes Chart 2 compares the natural modes of the key of C to their respective ***parallel major*** (explained in chapter 11 and the glossary) scales. It's really just a combination of Modes Chart 1 and a condensed version of Mode Worksheet #2. It differs in that the chromatic alterations are filled in, and that it has better pictures.

Modes Chart 2

Mode														
C Ionian	1	2	3	4	5	6	7	8						
D Dorian		1	2	♭3	4	5	6	♭7	8					
E Phrygian			1	♭2	♭3	4	5	♭6	♭7	8				
	C	**D**	**E**	**F**	**G**	**A**	**B**	**C**	**D**	**E**	**F**	**G**	**A**	**B**
F Lydian				1	2	3	#4	5	6	7	8			
G Mixolydian					1	2	3	4	5	6	♭7	8		
A Aeolian						1	2	♭3	4	5	♭6	♭7	8	
B Locrian							1	♭2	♭3	4	♭5	♭6	♭7	8

Now try this in the chart below: rearrange the modes in order of most raised notes to the most lowered notes. This could be described as the natural modes in a progression from "brightest" to "darkest." That is, raising tones makes a mode subjectively "brighter sounding," and lowering tones makes a mode sound "darker." This is a great way of conceptualizing the progression of the sound of the modes.

On the second line, write the major scale degree (Roman numerals, again) which is the tonic of the mode. On the third line, write the mode's tonic (note)—use the modes derived from the key of C major for this exercise.

Modes From "Brightest" to "Darkest"

Altered Notes:	1 #	All ♮	1 ♭	2 ♭s	3 ♭s	4 ♭s	5 ♭s
Name:	______	Ionian	______	______	______	______	______
Degree Number:	____	I	____	____	____	____	____
Tonic:	____	C	____	____	____	____	____

What relationship do you see between each successive tonic on line three? Specifically, what is the interval separating each tonic? Got it? Yes?! Surprised? No!? Good! Yes?

Let me point out just a couple of odd tidbits about several modes. In Phrygian, all *major intervals* of the major scale are lowered and are now minor; perfect intervals are left untouched. Also, Lydian is the only mode with a *raised* interval.

After going through the modes, try writing out some scales and modes so you can become a true modal monster:

E Mixolydian	E F# G# A B C# D E
F Dorian	....
B Locrian	....
A♭ Lydian	....
D Phrygian	....
D♭ Aeolian	....
F Phrygian	....
F# Locrian	....
B Mixolydian	....
B♭ Ionian	....
A Dorian	....
E♭ Lydian	....
G Aeolian	....
D♭ Ionian	....
C Locrian	....
E♭ Dorian	....
E Lydian	....
F# Aeolian	....
A Locrian	....
B♭ Phrygian	....
D♭ Lydian	....

Notation Space for True Modal Monsters

E Mixolydian

A Dorian

F Dorian

E♭ Lydian

B Locrian

G Aeolian

A♭ Lydian

D♭ Ionian

D Phrygian

C Locrian

D♭ Aeolian

E♭ Dorian

F Phrygian

E Lydian

F# Locrian

F# Aeolian

B Mixolydian

A Locrian

B♭ Ionian

B♭ Phrygian

So, the distinguishing features of the natural modes are summarized below—again, as compared to the major scale. Think of these as two "aerial views" of the modes. The left-hand list shows the natural modes listed in the order you get by reassigning the role of tonic to each successive note of the major scale. The right-hand list shows the modes in the order of most raised notes to most lowered notes—or "brightest to darkest." Notice that looking at the modes in this second way reveals a similarity to looking at the keys "in order," in that each successive alteration—shown in **bold**— (analogous to the newest added accidental in the case of keys) is *kept* as new ones are added.

I've found that an effective way to practice the modes on an instrument is in an order based in some way on the "brightest to darkest" model. For example, play the seven modes from Lydian to Locrian, for each note of the chromatic scale. If you can do this comfortably, you will be very well prepared to embark on a rewarding career as a moody modal mogul.

Seriously, modes serve—among other things—as a great jumping-off point for improvisation. They provide something to grab with your *brain* (use this mode for that type of chord, use this other mode for that other type of chord)—until your *ear* takes over and directs the ball game ("this is the sound I want right now"). This is explained further in "Scale/Mode Choices in Improvisation," in chapter 29. Here come the charts.

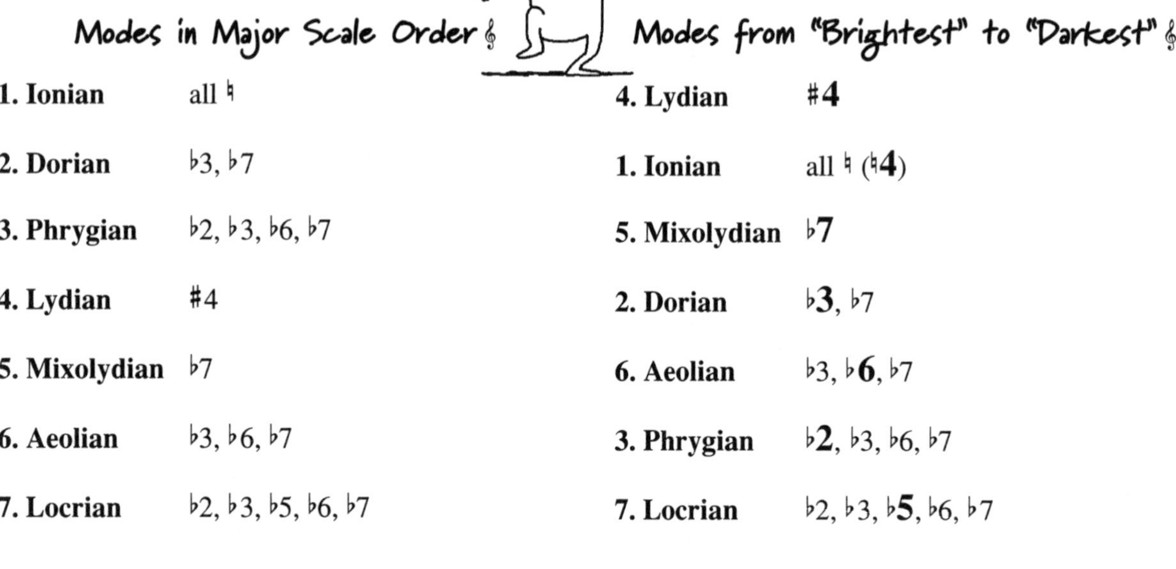

Modes in Major Scale Order 𝄞

Mode	Alterations
1. Ionian	all ♮
2. Dorian	♭3, ♭7
3. Phrygian	♭2, ♭3, ♭6, ♭7
4. Lydian	♯4
5. Mixolydian	♭7
6. Aeolian	♭3, ♭6, ♭7
7. Locrian	♭2, ♭3, ♭5, ♭6, ♭7

Modes from "Brightest" to "Darkest" 𝄞

Mode	Alterations
4. Lydian	**♯4**
1. Ionian	all ♮ (**♮4**)
5. Mixolydian	**♭7**
2. Dorian	**♭3**, ♭7
6. Aeolian	♭3, **♭6**, ♭7
3. Phrygian	**♭2**, ♭3, ♭6, ♭7
7. Locrian	♭2, ♭3, **♭5**, ♭6, ♭7

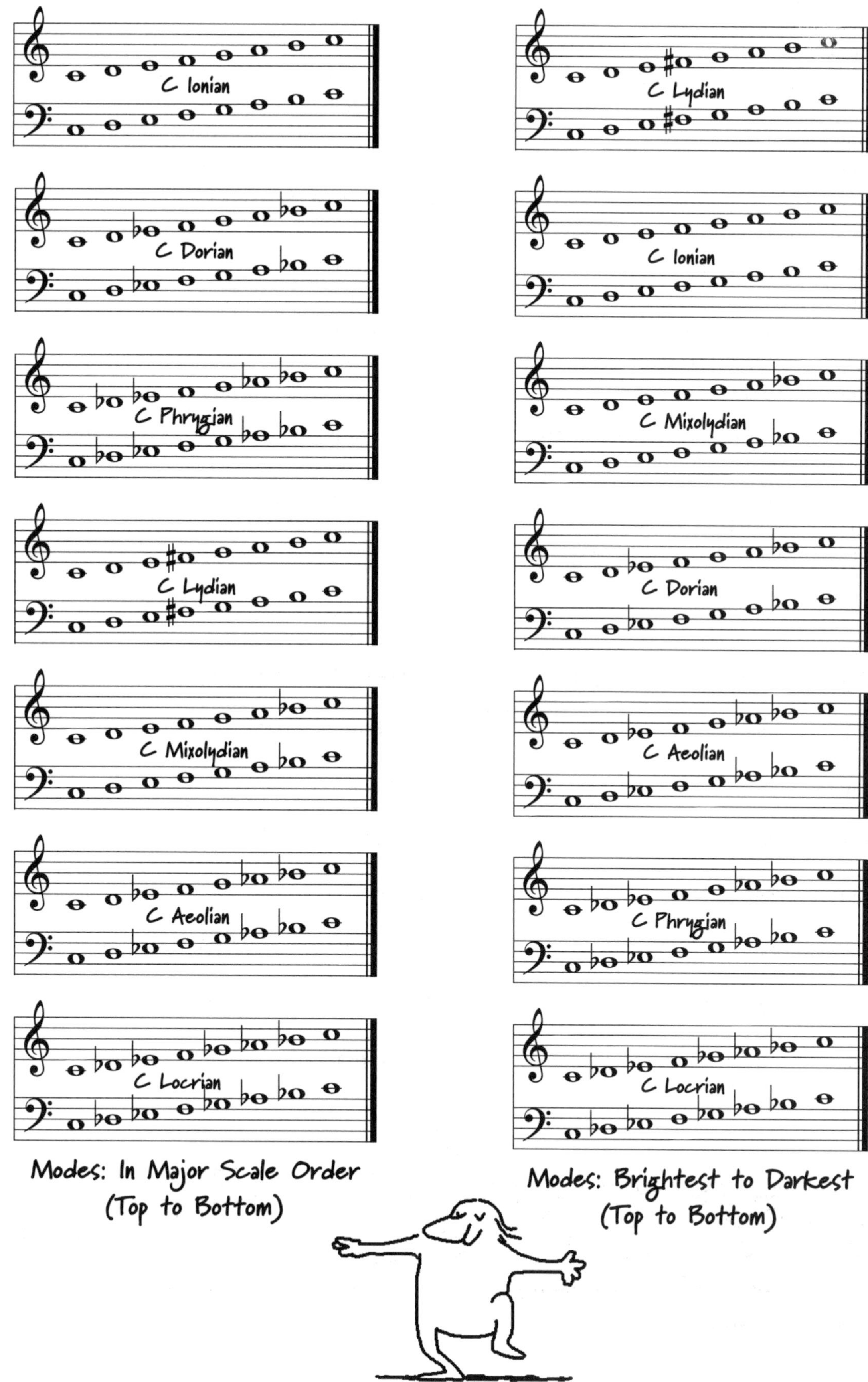

Modes: In Major Scale Order (Top to Bottom)

Modes: Brightest to Darkest (Top to Bottom)

Summary of the Modal Discovery Process

Here is the process we've used to become familiar with modes.

1. For each mode, take a major scale and move the tonics one note higher. This defines modes according to degrees of a major scale redefined as tonics. Using this method, the modes occur in order of "tonics ascending the major scale."

2. Compare each mode with the major scale beginning on the same tonic. This defines modes according to how they differ from the major scale beginning on the same tonic. The modes are still in order of tonics ascending the major scale.

3. ***Transpose*** modes such that they all begin on the same tonic. This enables the player to hear modes as modes, rather than a major scale beginning on various notes of the scale. The modes are *still* in order of tonics ascending major scale.

4. Reorganize the order of modes from "tonics ascending major scale" to "brightest to darkest." Notice that tonics move in fifths. Continue to play all of them beginning on the same tonic. Notice the gradual darkening of the modes.

Staff Paper for Your Scrawling Pleasure

The modes we've learned so far are collectively known as the "***natural modes***." Again, "natural modes" refers to the *modes derived from major scales*. You can create modes from any scale. A scale has *as many modes as it has notes*. Modes from scales other than the major scale (such as the harmonic minor, or pentatonics, which are introduced next) can sound quite interesting.

Chapter 22~ Pentatonic and Blues Scales

Pentatonic Scales

What: A "***pentatonic scale***" merely means any "five note scale." In Western music though, two are by far the most common. They are the ***major pentatonic***, and the ***minor pentatonic***. Though it may not at first be immediately apparent, they are *pentatonic versions* of the *relative major and minor.* You can see most of a C major scale in the C major pentatonic, and most of an A natural minor scale in the A minor pentatonic scale.

Why are they important? Look and listen for, and *use* these scales especially in rock, blues, and Chinese (!) music.

Major Pentatonic	1	2	3		5	6		(8)
C Major Pentatonic 𝄞	C	D	E		G	A		(C)

Minor Pentatonic	1		♭3	4	5		♭7	(8)
A Minor Pentatonic 𝄞	A		C	D	E		G	(A)

These pentatonic scales' characteristic sound comes from their having two minor third intervals (in parentheses in the example below), and no half-steps whatsoever, as opposed to the major scale, for instance, with its whole- and half-steps only.

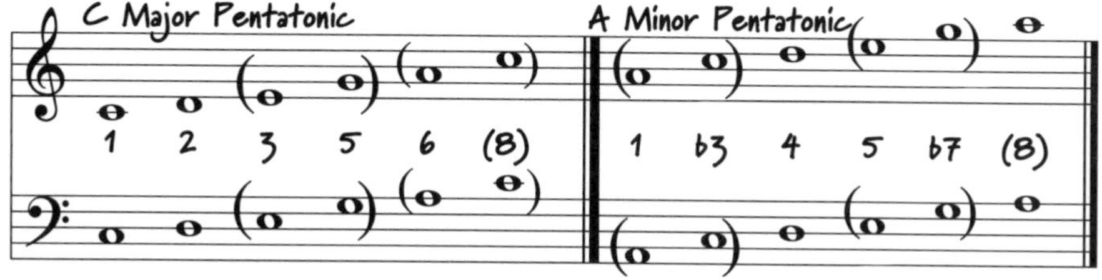

C Major and A Minor Pentatonic Scales

The Blues Scale

The ***blues scale*** is derived by adding a "blue note" to the minor pentatonic scale. This blue note is the ♯4 or ♭5, and is a tritone away from the tonic.

Blues	1	♭3	4	♯4 (♭5)	5	♭7	(8)
C Blues 𝄞	C	E♭	F	F♯ (G♭)	G	B♭	(C)

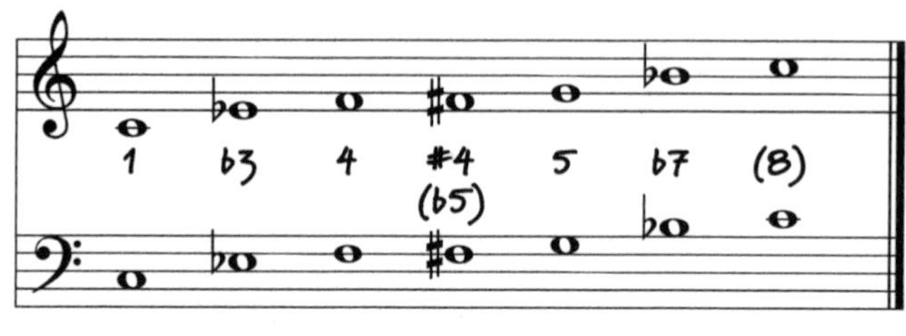

C Blues Scale

The *blue note* gives the blues scale its characteristic bluesy sound. In blues contexts, this sound is furthered by the rubbing of the blues scale's minor third against the major third of the tonic chord. By the way, notice that *none* of the thirds in the *I*, *IV*, and *V* chords, are present in the blues scale. Ah, more bluesy rubbing!

Further, *all* of the notes *in between* the fourth and fifth degrees are fair game in blues-based music. By this, I mean ***microtonal*** (smaller than a half-step) *notes*. Wind and guitar players love to bend these notes so the pitch is somewhere (anywhere) between the fourth and the fifth. Piano players, unable to bend notes, simulate the effect by playing clusters of the fourth, raised fourth, and fifth, in any combination. If you play an instrument that can bend notes, these, as well as from ♭3 to ♮3, and 6 to ♭7, are a great place to begin. You will surely recognize the sound!

Finally, try using this C blues scale with a blues progression in E♭. This is (you already knew?) actually an E♭ major pentatonic scale with a ♭3 added. It's a more major, less bluesy—but still bluesy enough (!)—sound, and was used to great effect by earlier blues/jazz crossover players. Enjoy.

Now try writing out some scales. Be Brave, or B♭! A

C blues	C E♭ F F# G B♭ C
F# blues	....
B♭ harmonic minor	....
G blues	....
F natural minor	....
D blues	....
A♭ melodic minor	....
F blues	....
E♭ melodic minor	....
B melodic minor	....
B♭ blues	....
E natural minor	....
F natural minor	....
F# harmonic minor	....
D♭ major pentatonic	....
D minor pentatonic	....
F major pentatonic	....
A major pentatonic	....
E♭ minor pentatonic	....
G♭ major pentatonic	....
A blues	....
C# blues	....
G harmonic minor	....

Chapter 23~ More Scales

Who: Jazz improvisers, jazz and classical composers, and those possessing an insatiable scalar appetite should read and learn this chapter. Others may browse or safely skip to the next chapter. If you elect to bypass this chapter for now, I hope ya'll'll come back soon, ya heah?!?! There is a lot of good to be reaped from these next pages!

"Artificial" or "Unnatural" Modes

What: "Artificial" or "unnatural" modes or scales can be defined as any scale or mode that alters or disturbs the relationship of whole-steps and half-steps found in the major scale, rather than just shifting the tonic of the scale up or down. These scales and modes sound spicier than their "natural" brothers and sisters.

Why these and not others? There are plenty more artificial modes—in fact there are whole books devoted solely to scale permutations. These are just a few to get you started. Check out these bananas[20], especially good for improvising over m7♭5 chords:

Locrian ♮6	1	♭2	♭3	4	♭5	6	♭7	(8)
C Locrian ♮6 𝄞	C	D♭	E♭	F	G♭	A	B♭	(C)

Locrian ♮2 (Aeolian ♭5)	1	2	♭3	4	♭5	♭6	♭7	(8)
C Locrian ♮2 𝄞	C	D	E♭	F	G♭	A♭	B♭	(C)

Locrian ♮2/♮6 (Dorian ♭5)	1	2	♭3	4	♭5	6	♭7	(8)
C Locrian ♮2/♮6 𝄞	C	D	E♭	F	G♭	A	B♭	(C)

Lydian ♭7 is best known for use over jazz substitute V^7 chords. Look for "sub five" chords in chapter 20.

Lydian ♭7	1	2	3	#4	5	6	♭7	(8)
C Lydian ♭7 𝄞	C	D	E	F#	G	A	B♭	(C)

20 (bananas is Italian for "artificial" or "unnatural" modes) ...just kidding.

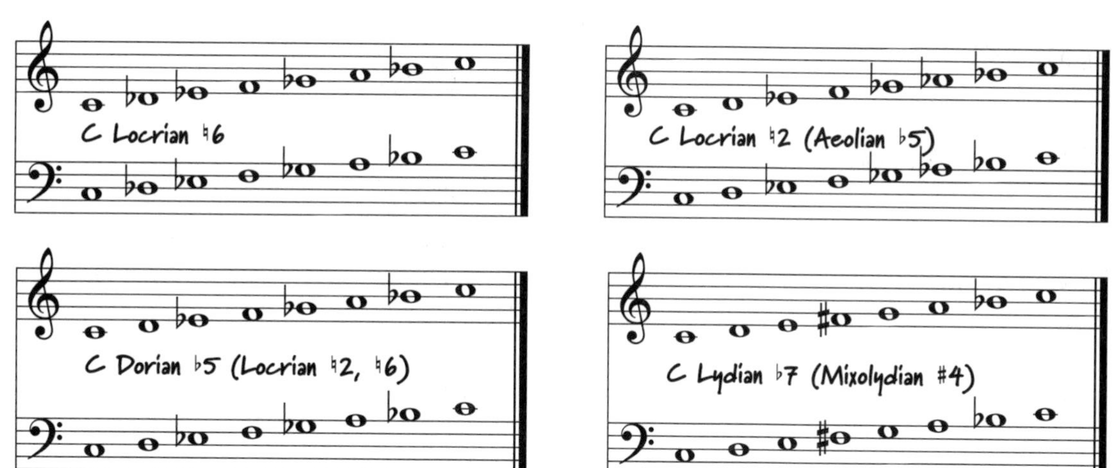

A Handful of Artificial Modes

The ***"Jazz Altered" scale*** includes the notes of the "dominant seventh skeleton" (1, 3, ♭7) and all possible *altered* ***tensions***. *Tensions* include 9, 11, and 13 (see chapter 24). *Altered tensions* include ♭9, #9, ♭5 (#11), and +5 (rarely spelled as ♭13). The ♭9, #9 can also be spelled ♭2 and ♭3 for our current scalar purposes. The "Altered" scale is useful for improvising over "altered" chords (see chapter 25), which are common enough in jazz.

"Jazz Altered" Scale	1	♭2	#2	3	#4	#5	♭7	(8)
Enharmonic Spellings	1	♭9	#9	3	#11	♭13	♭7	(8)
C Altered Scale 𝄞	C	D♭	E♭	E	F#	G#	B♭	(C)

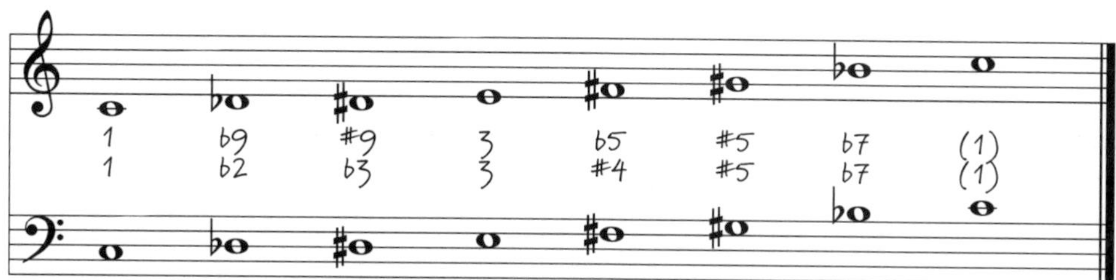

C "Jazz Altered" Scale

Notice how scales that include both large intervals (major third or larger) and small intervals (minor second) have a pronounced exotic sound to most Western ears. You'll hear these scales called various middle-Eastern sounding names.

Lydian ♭3 ♭6	1	2	♭3	#4	5	♭6	7	(8)
C Lydian ♭3 ♭6 𝄞	C	D	E♭	F#	G	A♭	B	(C)
Phrygian ♮3/♮7 𝄞	1	♭2	3	4	5	♭6	7	(8)
C Phrygian ♮3/♮7	C	D♭	E	F	G	A♭	B	(C)

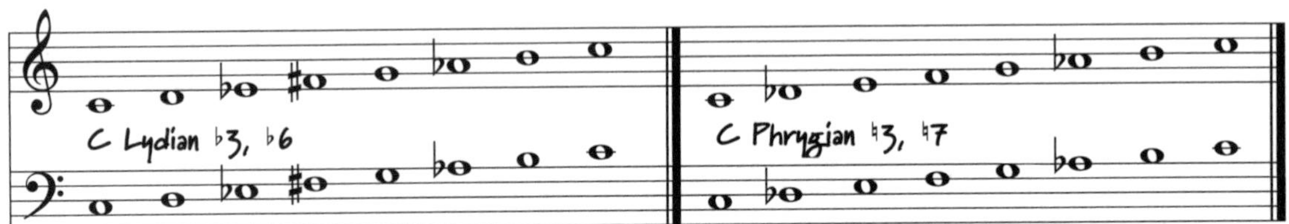

More Artificial Modes

Phrygian ♮3, the fifth mode of the harmonic minor scale, is known as "Ahava Raba" or "freygish" by Klezmer players.

"Exotic" Pentatonics

Both of these send images of Indonesia wafting through my mind. How 'bout you? I hope it's a well made waft, though, because it's a wong waft wide to Indonesia.

Here's a more exotic sounding pentatonic than the standard major and minor pentatonic:

Biff's Exotic Pentatonic	1	2		#4	5		7	(8)
C Example 𝄞	C	D		F#	G		B	(C)

…and another, which is actually just a mode of the preceding scale, starting on *its* fifth:

Betty-Sue-Alvin's Pent…	1		3	4	5		7	(8)
C Example 𝄞	C		E	F	G		B	(C)

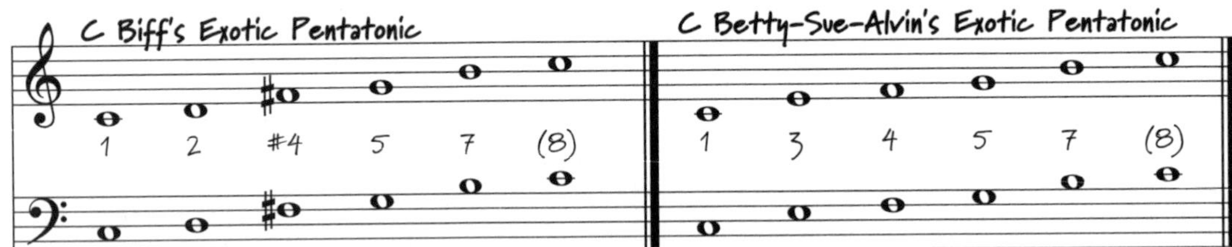

Exotic Pentatonic Scales

Whole-Tone and Diminished Scales

What: ***Whole-tone*** (whole-step) ***scales*** and ***diminished scales*** are different animals from anything covered thus far, in that they are constructed of modules, or patterns, of *consistent size*. This makes these scales ***symmetrical***. This symmetry gives them their characteristic unstable sound… and makes them harder to sing and hear accurately. This is in sharp contrast to the relatively mottled pattern of half-steps and whole-steps (and larger intervals) and comparatively stable sound that we've found in other scales thus far.

Whole-tone and diminished scales are built around, or at least contain, the augmented triad and diminished seventh chord, respectively. They interact first and foremost with these chords. The whole-tone scale, as its name implies, is made up of all whole-steps. The diminished scales are made up of alternating whole-steps and half-steps or alternating half-steps and whole-steps. These alternating whole-steps and half-steps form the modules of which I spoke in the previous paragraph.

Why: These scales are vital in jazz and classical music of the twentieth century.

In the case of these particular scales, the major scale becomes a bit unwieldy as a model. It's easier simply to build them from their constituent modules.

Diminished Scales

"whole-step/half-step" Dim. Scale module of alternating whole-steps and half-steps

C w/h Diminished Scale 𝄞 C D E♭ F G♭ A♭ A B (C)

"half-step/whole-step" Dim. Scale module of alternating half-steps and whole-steps

C h/w Diminished Scale 𝄞 C D♭ E♭ E F♯ G A B♭ (C)

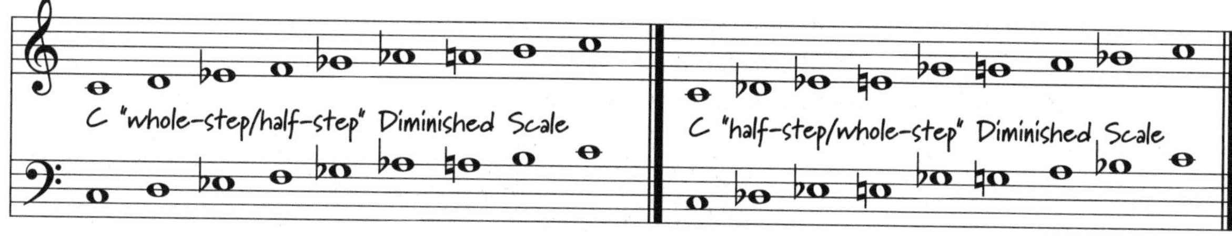

Diminished Scales

Both of these scales contain the (enharmonically spelled) tonic diminished seventh chord. All the other notes in each scale spell the ii°7 and ♭ii°7 chords, respectively. Another way to think of it is that each scale contains the tonic °7 chord and all the notes a whole-step higher in the case of the "whole-step/half-step" scale, and a half-step higher in the case of the "half-step/whole-step" scale.

These two scales are merely *transposed modes of each other*. The modal offset is by one scale degree, and the transposition is by a half-step. This is immediately apparent upon comparing the C w/h diminished Scale above with a B h/w diminished scale.

B h/w Diminished Scale 𝄞 B C D E♭ F G♭ A♭ A (B)

B "half-step/whole-step" Diminished Scale

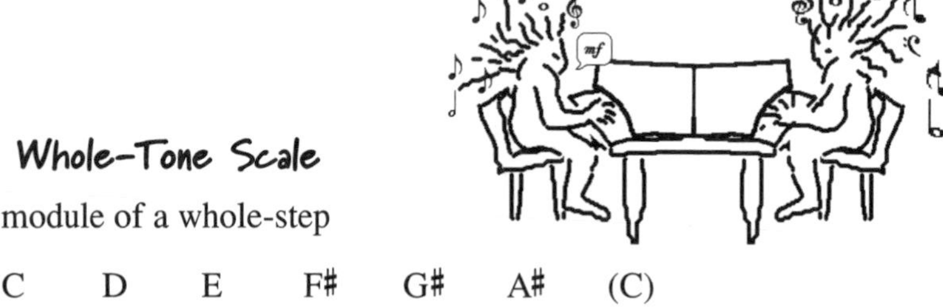

Whole-Tone Scale

Whole-Tone Scale module of a whole-step

C Whole-Tone Scale 𝄞 C D E F# G# A# (C)

The unstable sound of these scales can be additionally explained by the prominence of the already unstable ***tritone*** (remember the tritone?). I count four tritones in the whole-tone scale and *five* in each of the two diminished scales. 𝄞

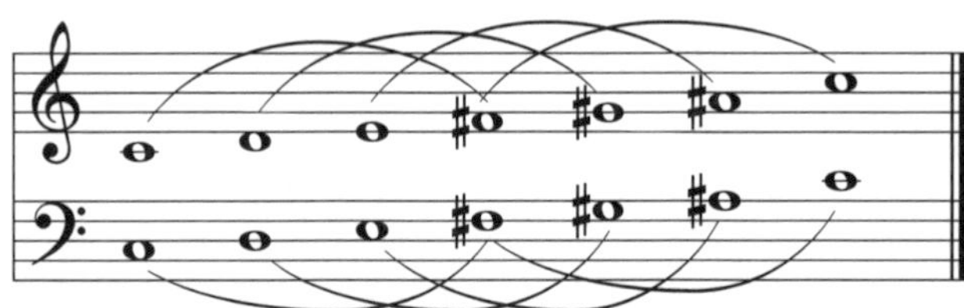

C Whole-Tone Scale with Tritones Marked

Here is yet a third explanation of these scales' unstable sound. They, like their corresponding chords (augmented triads and diminished sevenths, respectively), are *symmetrical*, as follows: in the case of the whole-tone scale, any note can be considered the tonic, whereas in the diminished scales, every other note can be the tonic. Wow.

We can use the tritone as the foundation-stone of another, even slicker way to conceive of these somewhat aberrant scales. This is in terms of a larger module beginning on the tonic, followed by the *same module* beginning a tritone (abbreviated "TT") higher, finally capped off by the high tonic. (In the case of the "w/h" diminished scale, this module consists of the *first four notes of a minor scale*. This makes it even easier!) I find this method to be the easiest way to think of the diminished scales.

Tritone-Based Modules in Whole-Tone and Diminished Scales

"w/h" Dim. Scale:	1	2	♭3	4	TT1	TT2	TT♭3	TT4	(1)
"h/w" Dim. Scale:	1	♭2	♭3	3	TT1	TT♭2	TT♭3	TT3	(1)
Whole-Tone Scale:		1	2	3	TT1	TT2	TT3		(1)

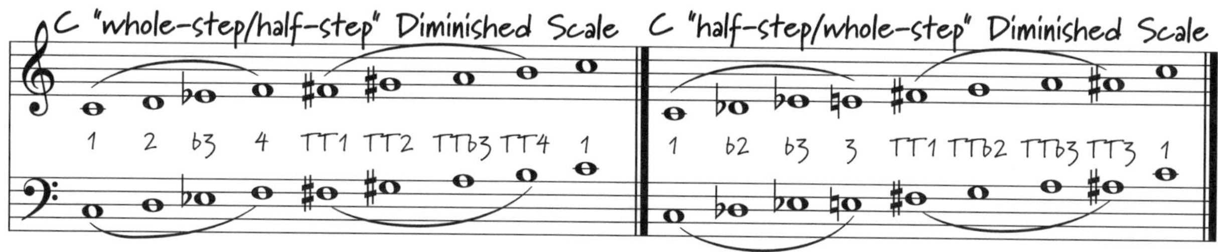

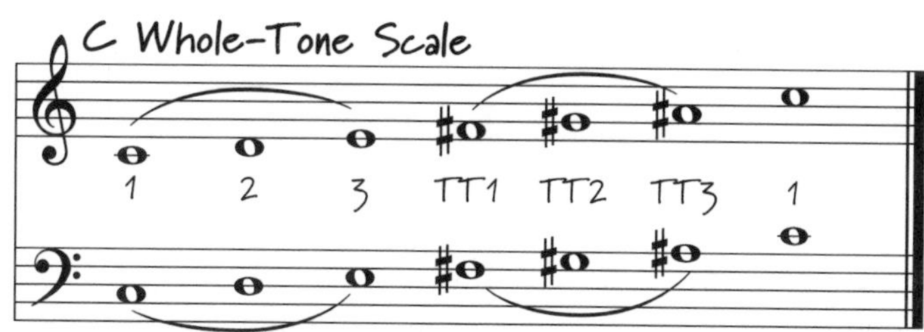

Diminished and Whole-Tone Scales: Larger Modules

For the improviser or composer, the whole-tone and diminished scales are extremely useful in a wide variety of situations. For example, $C^{7\flat9}$ ("seven flat nine" chords will be introduced later) can be looked at as a $D\flat^{\circ7}$ with a missing root, suggesting the use of the D♭ diminished scale. Also, a C+ or a $C^{7\sharp11}$ or $C^{7\flat5}$ suggests a C whole-tone scale, or a wide variety of whole-tone scale or ***arpeggio*** patterns such as C, D, E, G#, D, E, F#, A#, and so on, or even C, E, G#, D, F#, A#, etc., as well as their descending counterparts. The beauty of these scales for the improviser is that facility in just a handful of whole-tone and diminished scales yields great returns, since the symmetrical nature of both scales creates exact replicates. For instance, the C, E♭, G♭, and A diminished scales are all the exact same scale with the tonic moved. This is also the case with the C, D, E, F#, A♭, and B♭ whole-tone scales.

Actually, because of the symmetry of these scales, there are only two different whole-tone, and three different diminished scales.

Modes from Mercury

Fine Print: Do you, scale fanatic, dare to ask me about Gustav Holst's "artificial scale" from the Mercury movement of *The Planets Suite?!?* Yes?! Rest assured; ye shall not be disappointed! Notice that this is "merely" a whole-tone scale with 4 and TT4 added:

Holst's "Mercury Mode"	1	2	3	4	TT1	TT2	TT3	TT4	(1)
B♭ Mercury Mode 𝄞	B♭	C	D	E♭	E	F#	G#	A	(B♭)

More Fine Print: I got an idea from Holst's "Mercury Mode." (The name's my own—I had to call it something!) I asked myself, "what would happen if I 'inverted' the process?" Instead of using the first four notes of a major scale, what would happen if I used the *last four notes* of a major scale instead? That's how I ended up with "Inverted Mercury Mode." I like it. Try "Mercury Mode" ascending, and "Inverted Mercury Mode" descending… or vice versa, if you are particularly bold!

"Inverted Mercury Mode"	1	TT5	TT6	TT7	TT1	5	6	7	(1)
B♭ Inverted Mercury Mode 𝄞	B♭	B	C#	D#	E	F	G	A	(B♭)

Holst's "Mercury Mode"
1 2 3 4 TT1 TT2 TT3 TT4 (1)
Edly's "Inverted Mercury Mode"
1 TT5 TT6 TT7 TT8 5 6 7 (8)

Holst's "Mercury," and Edly's "Inverted Mercury" Modes

Even Finer Print: This could go on for a long time, but I just want to get you rolling. You're probably rolling by now—perhaps rolling over on the couch to find your glasses, or perhaps just rolling your eyes. I hope that this section may prove useful to some seeking to extend their understanding of scales beyond the norm. (We love ya', Norm!) In any case, by this point you know *more* than enough to construct all kinds of scales, and hopefully have the flexibility and audacity to do so. If that's the case, then I have accomplished my goal in this section.

Lastly, don't forget to use your ears! They are the final judges. Now all you have to do is to learn to play these scales, as well as the ones you come up with, and learn where to use them. The first is up to you, and the second… well, this book gets you started, but to go even farther, I'd suggest you seek out a book dealing specifically with improvisation.

Good luck… and remember always to read the fine print.

Chapter 24~ Chords: 9ths, 11ths, and 13ths

Why: Chords get richer as more notes are added. ***Extensions*** such as ninths, elevenths, and thirteenths are vital for any jazz-based music. Basic rock could *probably* get by without ninths, but blues would suffer. And so would any even slightly well-rounded musician.

Who: If you are reading this book, then I assume this includes *you*.

Ninth Chords

Ninth chords appear generously in blues, and also in jazz, where seventh chords are often considered a bit bare and lacking in spice.

Why not call a ninth a second, an eleventh a fourth, and a thirteenth a sixth, since each higher extension is the same interval as the corresponding smaller interval, merely extended by an octave?

Questions like this help keep teachers from becoming complacent. Keep 'em coming! The answer hearkens back to the fact that chords are built of stacked thirds. From each chord-tone to the next higher one is a third (from root to third, third to fifth, fifth to seventh, seventh to ninth, and so on). Each lower chord tone is *retained* as the chord is built upwards. Notice that ninths *include the seventh*, as well as the root, third, and fifth. Elevenths include the ninth, as well as the other lower chord tones.

At least, in theory. Unfortunately, in practice, there are exceptions, which you will see below. For example, the standard (dominant) eleventh chord omits the third, and very often the fifth, too. In this case, including the third would make the chord too dissonant for its usual role, and including the fifth tends to muddy things up unnecessarily. These common practice exceptions will become second nature as you get used to using these chords. For now, take note of them as you scan through.

In the course of jazz history, chordal accompaniment gradually moved from simple triads and occasional sevenths to higher extensions and chromatically altered chords. One way to think of this is as 'harmony absorbing melody': accompanying chords taking on notes that formerly appeared in the melody. The $^{7\#9}$ chord is a great example of this: an early blues or jazz soloist playing a ♭3rd note over a major or seventh chord in the accompaniment eventually led to the development of the $^{7\#9}$ chord played by the chordal instrument. (Note, though, that the effect of a note added to a chord can be different from that of the same chord and note split between two different instruments. Listen for this in early blues and jazz.)

Some Ninth Chords

Name (chord type)	Abbreviation	Spelling					C Sample 𝄞				
major 9th	maj 9, Δ9	1	3	5	7	9	C	E	G	B	D
(dominant) 9th	9	1	3	5	♭7	9	C	E	G	B♭	D
minor 9th	m9, – 9	1	♭3	5	♭7	9	C	E♭	G	B♭	D
9th, flat 5	9 ♭5	1	3	♭5	♭7	9	C	E	G♭	B♭	D
augmented 9th	+9, aug 9	1	3	#5	♭7	9	C	E	G#	B♭	D
suspended 9th	sus 9	1	4	5	♭7	9	C	F	G	B♭	D
six, nine	6/9	1	3	5	6	9	C	E	G	A	D
minor six, nine	m6 9, – 6/9	1	♭3	5	6	9	C	E♭	G	A	D
7th, flat 9th	7 ♭9	1	3	5	♭7	♭9	C	E	G	B♭	D♭
seventh, sharp 9th	7 #9	1	3	5	♭7	#9	C	E	G	B♭	D#
seventh, flat five, sharp 9th	7 ♭5 #9	1	3	♭5	♭7	#9	C	E	G♭	B♭	D#
aug. major 9th	maj 9+	1	3	#5	7	9	C	E	G#	B	D
minor, major 9th	– (maj 9), mM9	1	♭3	5	7	9	C	E♭	G	B	D

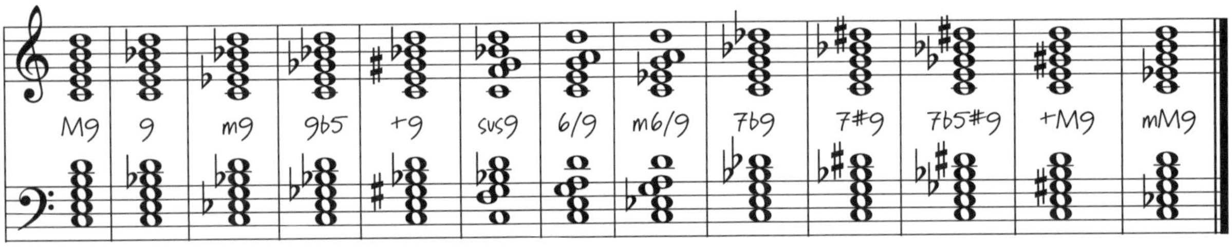

M9 9 m9 9♭5 +9 sus9 6/9 m6/9 7♭9 7#9 7♭5#9 +M9 mM9

Some Ninth Chords

About inverting the higher extensions (9ths, 11ths, and 13ths): as a *very* general rule, ninths, elevenths, and thirteenths tend to stay "higher" rather than "lower" in a voicing. They tend to muddy things up if voiced too low in a chord. Refer to a book that deals with voicings for your specific instrument. Or even better, ask your teacher.

Diatonic Ninth Chords

If you understand diatonic sevenths, diatonic ninths should be no problem. See if you can figure them out yourself. Check the Answers chapter if you're unsure.

Diatonic Ninths: _____ _____ _____ _____ _____ _____ _____

Eleventh Chords

In real world usage, eleventh chords begin to get a bit quirky. Fear not; thirteenth chords finish the job. Elevenths and thirteenths are not for everybody. Hard-core folkies (are there any of you reading this book?), hard and thrash rockers, or anyone who doesn't feel particularly harmonically inspired at the moment … feel free to skip to chapter 25. For the rest of you, don't touch that dial, and read on!

Some Eleventh Chords

NAME (CHORD TYPE)	ABBREVIATION	SPELLING						C SAMPLE 𝄞					
(dominant) 11th	11	1		5	♭7	9	11	C		G	B♭	D	F
minor 11th	m11	1	♭3	5	♭7	9	11	C	E♭	G	B♭	D	F
major 9th, sharp 11	maj 9#11	1	3	5	7	9	#11	C	E	G	B	D	F#
9th #11	9 #11	1	3	5	♭7	9	#11	C	E	G	B♭	D	F#

- A sharp eleven is the same as a flat five (#11 = ♭5) (enharmonically spelled and displaced by an octave). The difference is that with any #11 chord, the ♮5 is retained, making the chord even richer than a ♭5 chord, where we lose the ♮5 to the ♭5. Try 'em; you'll see!
- For the most part, with 11th chords, you won't see a natural 11 with a major 3rd. It just doesn't come up in polite conversation. With a major 3rd, the 11 will be raised. With a natural 11, the (major) 3rd will be omitted. Therefore, a (dominant) 11th chord is basically the same as a suspended 9th chord.

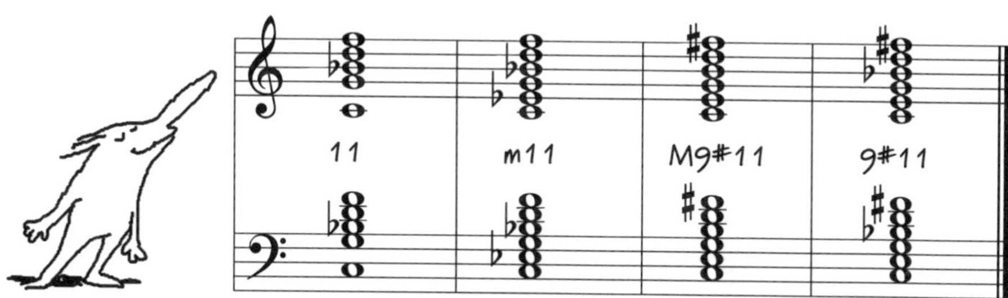

Some Eleventh Chords

A V^{11} chord mellows the magnetic pull of the *V* with a subtler *IV* flavor. In fact, the chord could be thought of as a *IV* chord over a *V* bass.

With a minor third, the eleventh, when present, is usually natural, although I suppose some wise-guy (myself, for instance) might use a #11, too. Stranger things have happened, though I can't say when.

There are plenty of other eleventh chords that are theoretically possible. They aren't frequently heard, though. Besides, by this point, you could probably figure out any new chords yourself. If not yet, then certainly in a couple of pages!

Thirteenth Chords

Lucky for you, and unlucky for teachers (me, for example), thirteenths are easier to play than to explain. They're quirky li'l buggers! In the end, the final judge is your keen ear, guided by your impeccable taste, and aided by common practice conventions. I will leave the ear and taste up to you, and will have to be satisfied to address only common practice.

Some Thirteenth Chords

Name (Chord Type)	Abbreviation	Spelling							C Sample 𝄞						
13th ❀	13	1	3		♭7	(9)		13	C	E		B♭	D		A
minor 13th	m13	1	♭3	5	♭7	9	11	13	C	E♭	G	B♭	D	F	A
11/13		1		5	♭7	9	11	13	C		G	B♭	D	F	A
major 13th ❀❀	M13/Maj 13	1	3	5	7	9		13	C	E	G	B	D		A
major 13th/#11	M13/#11	1	3	5	7	9	#11	13	C	E	G	B	D	F#	A
13/#11		1	3	5	♭7	9	#11	13	C	E	G	B♭	D	F#	A
minor 13th #11 ✗✗	m13/#11	1	♭3	5	♭7	9	#11	13	C	E♭	G	B♭	D	F#	A
13/#11/#9		1	3	5	♭7	#9	#11	13	C	E	G	B♭	D#	F#	A

❀ The fifth of the chord is sometimes omitted in some thirteenth chord voicings, the (dominant) thirteenth being a good example. While including the fifth doesn't sound particularly bad, its inclusion can also cloud the chord, adding bulk while adding little flavor. This depends on context, so use your ear and ask your teacher, and/or refer to a book specific to your instrument.

❀❀ Chances are good that major thirteenth chords only get invited to parties without the eleventh. Again, the problem is the *friction-filled* interval of a minor ninth from the major third to the eleventh. Don't take my word for this; try it yourself, and you'll see.

✗✗ Listen for this chord in your favorite soap opera soundtrack, when *she* comes home to find *him* with *another woman* (or vice versa).

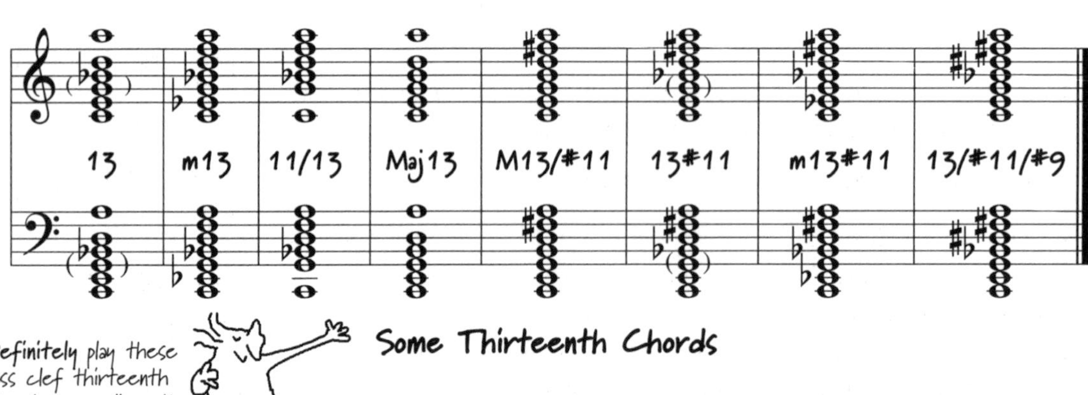

Some Thirteenth Chords

Definitely play these bass clef thirteenth chords, as well as the one on the next page, up an octave.

Chapter 25~
Chords: Summary and Exceptions

1. When building a chord upwards beyond a triad (an *extension*), all odd numbered notes on the ladder below are kept. 𝄞

Exception: "add" chords (add 9, or add #11, for instance), as the name implies, merely include the added note with the existing chord. *For example*: add^9 = 1, 3, 5, 9 (no 7!)

Exception: Some 11th and 13th chords often omit the 3rd and/or 5th, depending on the specific circumstance. Refer to chapter 24.

Exception: 6/9 chords substitute the 6th for any kind of seventh. Strange, but true.

C(add9) (no 7!) C11 (no 3!) C6/9 (no 7!)

Exceptions to the "Keep the Odd Numbers" Rule

2. All extensions (9ths, 11ths, and 13ths) are *unaltered*—that is, taken directly from the major scale—unless otherwise noted. *The only exception is the* **7th**, which causes a lot of confusion because it comes so low on the "chordal ladder." It should therefore be memorized (!) immediately. *The 7th is lowered* (a dominant 7th) *unless notated as maj7, in which case it is natural.* Once again, the *major 7th* (both the *interval*, and the *chord*) comes au naturel—unaltered—from the major scale! Unless "major seventh" is specified, use the ♭7th. *If this isn't clear to you, review* chapter 13.

The Chord Name Dictates the Contents

3. Don't be intimidated by the higher chord extensions. Often, the fancier the chord, the more completely the chord name dictates the contents. 𝄞

For example: 13 #9 #11 = 1 3 5 7 #9 #11 13 (Easy!!)

Edlytor's Note: It's again time to mention my admonition to bass clef readers: examples such as the one immediately to the right will sound *terrible* as written. Transpose your examples up an octave or more as necessary. I just couldn't stand the thought of ya'll painfully figuring out treble clef examples note by note. I'm sensitive that way.

4. Speaking of dominant sevenths, for now, suffice it to say that chords with a ♮3rd and a ♭7th (including 9ths, 11ths, and 13ths) usually serve some kind of *dominant function.* This means that they tend to resolve *down a fifth* (or up a fourth) or, in the case of jazz substitute V^7s, also *down a minor second.* See chapter 14 and chapter 20.

Exception: In blues, and blues-based styles, 7ths are pretty much added at will, and therefore serve other functions in addition to a dominant function.

5. Some chords (especially ones larger than triads) can often have more than one name. 𝄞

C6 or Am7 | B°7, D°7, F°7, A♭°7, or G♯°7 | F+, A+, C♯+, or D♭+ | Dm7♭5 or Fm6 | C7♭5, G♭7♭5, or F♯7♭5

A Chord Can Sometimes Have Several Possible Names

Together, the bass note and context of the chord progression determine the correct chord name. This is taken care of for you by the arranger and copyist, until you begin to write your own music. Then it falls upon your shoulders.

6. The notation "X/Y" means **X chord** on top of **Y bass note**. It's that simple. 𝄞

$\text{Fmaj}^7\text{sus/G}$ = Fmaj^7sus chord over a G bass. C/B♭ = C chord over B♭ bass.

Exception: "Δ" means "triad," and/or major triad, unless otherwise specified (unfortunately, it also is used sometimes to mean "major seventh"): 𝄞

F/GΔ = F triad over G triad. $\text{F\#m}^7$/GΔ = $\text{F\#m}^7$ over G maj triad

These are ***polychords***, explained more fully next.

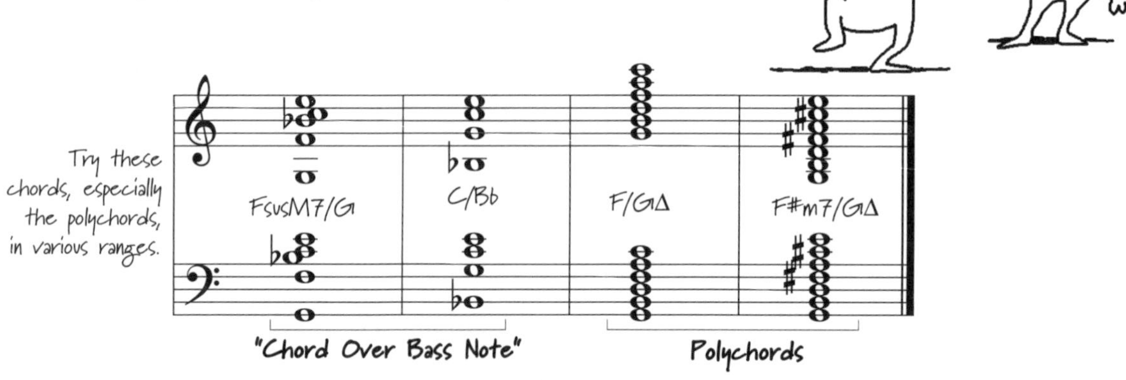

Slash Can Separate Chord and Bass or Indicate Polychords

A horizontal line is sometimes (and perhaps *better*) used instead of a slash. $\frac{\text{Fmaj}^7\text{sus}}{\text{G}}$ $\frac{\text{C}}{\text{B}\flat}$ $\frac{\text{F}}{\text{G}\Delta}$ $\frac{\text{F\#m}^7}{\text{G}\Delta}$

7. *Polychords* are two *chords* superimposed: one chord voiced above another. Sometimes it's easier to name a large chord as a polychord.

For example: F$^{6/9\sharp 11}$ is a mouthful! G/FΔ means the same thing. 𝄞 E♭m$^{6/9/11}$ is the same as Fm/E♭m. 𝄞 Note that the slash in E♭m$^{6/9/11}$ just separates the numbers visually; it *does not* mean E♭m^{6} *over* 9 *over* 11! (Thank goodness!)

Also in the previous example: Fm/E♭m means Fm over an E♭m *triad* even though there's no Δ (triad) symbol. Who ever heard of an E♭m *note*?

Be sure to voice the polychord high enough so that the bottom chord isn't muddy. Trust your ear! If your ear isn't trustworthy, then *train it!!* (Remember that the notation examples in this book are written on both clefs, and are not necessarily meant to be played on the octave written. The polychords written on the bass clef staff would need to be inverted higher to sound good.)

Polychords

8. Altered Chords: (abbreviated "alt") altered chords include 1, 3, ♭7, plus *any or every other altered extension tone* including ♭5, +5, ♭9, ♯9, and ♯11. … wonderfully hard-hitting; big bands love 'em, and so do I. Don't you?

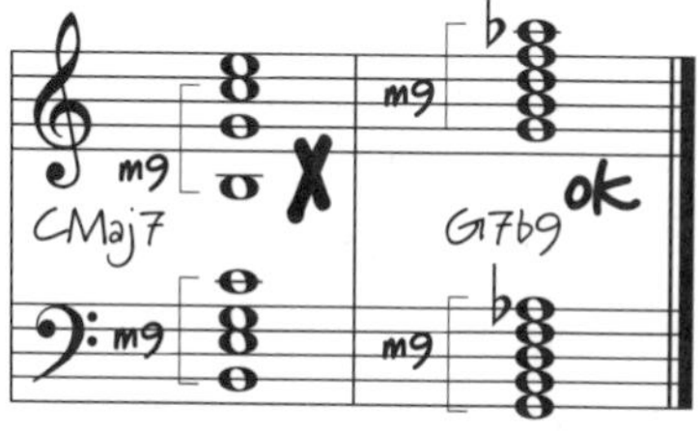

Minor Ninth Interval Do's and Don't's

9. A lowered note in a chord is sometimes notated with a dash (-).

Example: F$^{7-5}$ = F$^{7\flat 5}$ A♭$^{7-9}$ = A♭$^{7\flat 9}$

A raised note is sometimes notated with a "+."

Example: E^{7+9} = E$^{7\sharp 9}$ D♭$^{9+11}$ = D♭$^{9\sharp 11}$

The m$^{7\flat 5}$ chord is often called a half diminished 7th and abbreviated ø^{7}, but m$^{7\flat 5}$ is the preferred name and abbreviation. Again, you're at the mercy of the copyist or typesetter of the music you are reading.

10. When inverting and voicing chords, avoid, or use with care the *minor ninth interval* unless you know *why* you're using it. It's dissonant enough to be a bit taboo[21]. For example, this (ascending) voicing 𝄞 of a CM^{7} chord—B, E, G, C— might[22] be a bit too tense for a lounge ***gig*** (unless in the context of a descending bass line, for example) due to the minor ninth between B and C. People might spill their drinks in the piano. An exception to this "rule" is the $^{7\flat 9}$ chord, which elegantly accommodates this interval. 𝄞 (above)

11. A final reiteration: chord symbols are among the *least standardized* aspects of music notation. In the wild wild world of contemporary notation, you must be thinking, listening, and reading melodies in order to survive ("survive" is Tarzan talk for "to decipher chord symbols accurately, play well, and get re-hired for the ***gig***"). Stay on your toes; it's a harmonic ~~jingle~~—ahhh, *jungle* out there!

---

21 Sing 𝄆 "to be a bit taboo" 𝄇 five times fast using your favorite arpeggio!

22 Having said that, allow me to add that I personally **love** this voicing and have used it in my own music many times. But this book is **not** about what I like, but rather about common practice. Therefore, I had to include this precaution, or I'd have the music theory lawyers banging down my door.

Chord Building Practice

Try your hand at forming these chords, if you dare:

F7#9 ..... F A C E♭ G#

F#/Em .....

A♭m11 .....

D♭9#11 .....

G13 (no 11) .....

B♭m6/9 .....

Bmaj9#11 .....

Em (maj9) .....

Aº7 (add 9) .....

Fm6/9 .....

F/E♭m .....

A♭ #11 .....

Dm11 .....

E♭m13 .....

B° .....

E♭maj9#11 .....

F#maj9 .....

C#º7 (add 9) .....

E♭7♭5♭9 .....

Am/F# .....

Fm9♭5 .....

Gm9#11 .....

A♭+9 .....

F#m7♭5 .....

C#9♭5 .....

E♭+7♭9#11 .....

Fm11 .....

E♭m7♭5 .....

A♭m9/F .....

F#9+ .....

Cm13#11 .....

A7♭9 .....

Fm9♭5 .....

F#sus9♭5 .....

G+7#9#11 .....

Fm11♭5 .....

Did you notice that the Am/F# is the same chord as the F#m$^{7\flat5}$? You did? Oh, good. I was sure hoping you would. Pat yourself on the back, but be sure to stretch first—unless of course, you're already limber—perhaps from so many self-back-pats.

Another example of a chord with two names is the $^{7\flat5}$ chord. E♭$^{7\flat5}$, for example, is made up of the same notes as A7$^{\flat5}$. (Also notice the interval between the roots of these two chords!) The more you work with chords, the more you'll find associations like this.

Chord Building Practice for Readers

Chapter 26~
Diatonic Modal Chords

What? Major and minor scales have diatonic chords. So do modes. Further, each mode has characteristic chord progressions that reflect the mode's unique sound.

Why? The advantages of learning characteristic modal chord progressions are similar to the advantages of being able to recognize keys, scales, modes, and other components of music. They exist whether you're aware of them or not, and if you are aware of what to look for, then you're one step ahead.

Here's a reminder about notating chords built on chromatically altered (non diatonic) notes. An A♭ chord in the key of C, for example, would be *♭VI*—a major chord built on the lowered sixth degree. You'll also see it written *VI♭*, by the way, depending on who is doing the notating. I prefer the accidentals first, so there's no chance of getting them mixed up with the chord suffix.

In the chart below, the chords that particularly characterize each mode are in **bold**. These are debatable, but I tried to err on the conservative side instead of including five out of seven chords per mode. Here's the gist: in addition to the tonic chord, any chords (with the exception of the diminished chord) which contain the "newest altered note"[23] help to define the mode. Got it? Let's go! (By the way, notice that the tonic chord is always important in defining the modality.) 𝄞

Diatonic Modal Chords

Mode	Tonic	Supertonic	Mediant	Subdom.	Dominant	Submediant	Leading Tone
Lydian	**I**	**II**	iiim	#iv°	V	vim	**viim**
Ionian	**I**	iim	iiim	**IV**	**V**	vim	vii°
Mixolydian	**I**	iim	iii°	IV	**vm**	vim	**♭VII**
Dorian	**im**	**iim**	♭III	**IV**	vm	vi°	♭VII
Aeolian	**im**	**ii°**	♭III	**ivm**	vm	**♭VI**	♭VII
Phrygian	**i**	**♭II**	♭III	ivm	v°	♭VI	**♭viim**
Locrian	**i°**	♭II	**♭iiim**	ivm	**♭V**	♭VI	♭viim

23 Remember the modes "from brightest to darkest"? Reminder: moving one mode at a time from Lydian to Locrian, one note is altered (lowered) each time, and every alteration remains for the rest of the modes. The "newest altered notes" are Ionian's ♮4, Mixolydian's ♭7, Dorian's ♭3, Aeolian's ♭6, Phrygian's ♭2, and Locrian's ♭5.

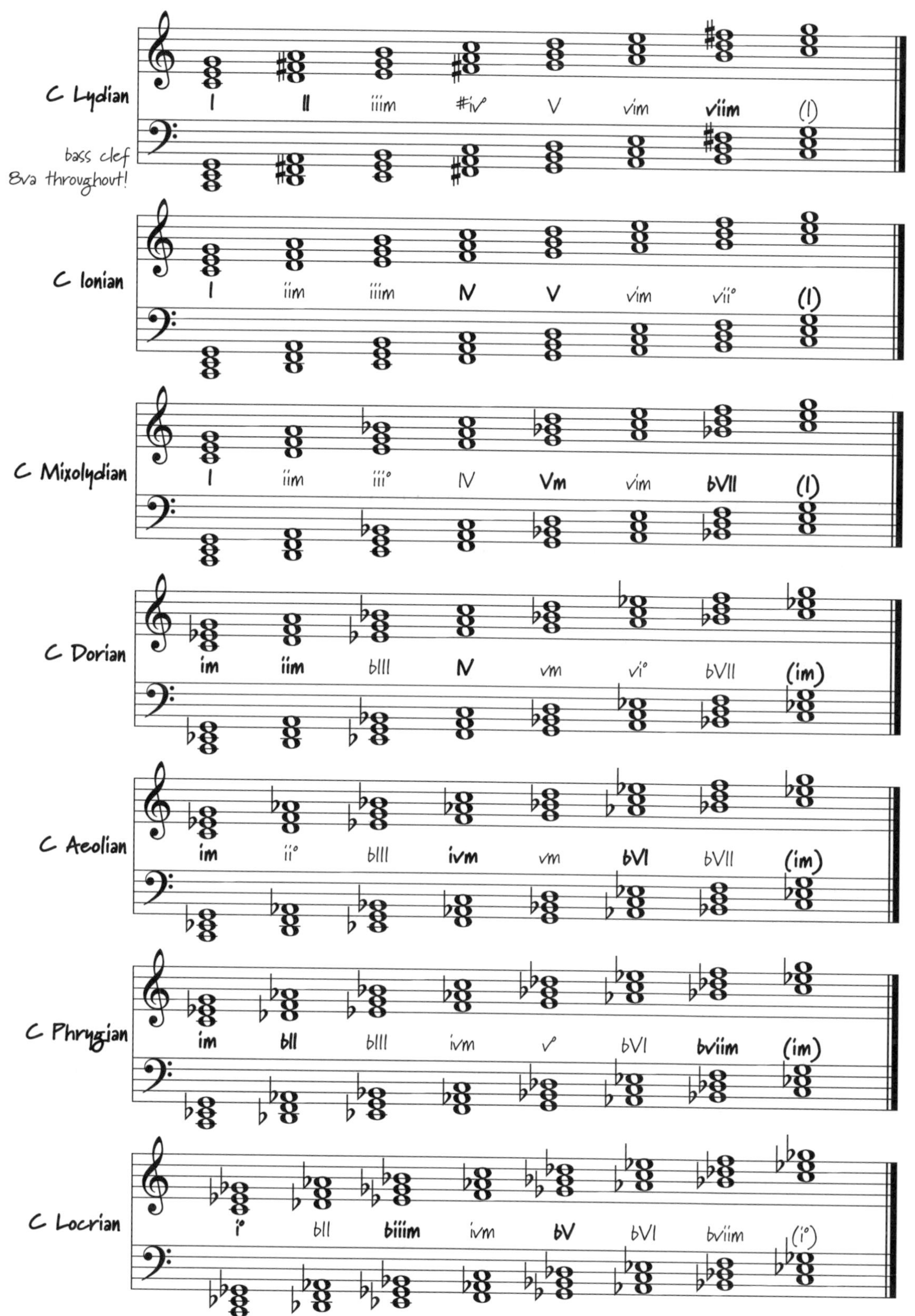

Modal Diatonic Chords—Brightest to Darkest (Characteristic Chords in Bold)

Here, then, is an only *slightly* subjective summary of the characteristic modal triads.

Characteristic Diatonic Modal Chords Summary

Ionian: I, IV, and V

Dorian: im, iim, and IV

Phrygian: i, ♭II, and ♭viim

Lydian: I, II, and viim

Mixolydian: I, vm, and ♭VII

Aeolian: im, ii°, ivm, and ♭VI

Locrian: i°, ♭iii, and ♭V

Put together some four bar chord progressions using the characteristic chords from each mode. If you play a "single line" instrument, use arpeggios instead. Can you *hear* the mode being clearly outlined by the notes/chords that you're playing? If not, I hope you will with time. Knowing what something is, and having a name for it, helps you recognize it when you see it or hear it.

Listen for modes and fragments of modes. You may be surprised how often you find them when you know what to look for, and actually *do* look!

Looking at the diatonic Locrian chords, it is easy to see just why you don't often run into pure Locrian music: the tonic chord is diminished and therefore unstable, and the "dominant chord" is built on the root a tritone away from the tonic. These two things make Locrian a challenging mode.

Modal Chord Functions

The most significant way in which modal harmony functions differently from tonal harmony is in the case of the ♭*VII* and ♭*viim* chords. Here's a really handy summary: in modes with a lowered seventh, the triad built on that very lowered seventh often acts as an "alternate dominant." In other words, it often pulls towards the tonic just as the *V* or *vm* chord does.

Chapter 27~ Blues Structure Part II

Why? The twelve bar blues has been used by so many composers as a springboard for many types of popular music. Put a spring in your step by learning as many variations of the twelve bar blues as possible.

There are whole books written on the blues, and this chapter is not by any means exhaustive, but these progressions will get you started. The variations are infinite, so recombine these at will. The progressions beyond the first several have much more to do with jazz than blues itself, as any *real* blues fan would be quick to point out!

These are not dictates of what you should do, but rather, descriptions of what is commonly done.

- As I've already said, thinking in non-key-specific terms can be very helpful when it comes to transposing chord progressions. Perhaps even more important, thinking in non-key-specific terms shows clearly *how* similar chord progressions occurring in different keys are similar, whereas this is harder to see in key-specific notation.
- I notated all of these in non-key-specific terms as well as in the key of C. For the sake of simplicity, secondary dominants and friends are notated *diatonically* (i.e., VI^7 instead of $V^7/V/V$). Use your knowledge of harmonic movement to figure out the chords' functions.
- Chromatic alterations (such as $+^5$, or $^{7\#9}$, or making a m^7 into a $m^{7\flat5}$) will make any progression sound jazzier. For a bluesier sound, simplify or omit these. Also again, in bluesy contexts, add dominant seventh and ninth chords at will.

Twelve bar blues number 1 and 2 have a ragtimey, honky-tonk flavor. Numbers 3 and 4 are decidedly jazzy, and number 5 is only included for you to use as a springboard to come up with your own (closely or distantly) blues-based chord progressions. Remember, these are not dictates of what you should or must do, but rather descriptions of what is commonly done. Once you understand these, you can move on to creating your own variations. Maybe you will come up with a new standard!

1. With standard iv^{m6}, chromatic descent and secondary dominant turnaround

I / / /	IV / / /	I / / /	I^7 / / /
C	F	C	C^7
IV / / /	iv^{m6} / / /	I I VII ♭VII	VI^7 / / /
F	F^{m6}	C C B B♭	A^7
II^7 / / /	V^7 / / /	I / VI^7 /	II^7 / V^7 /
D^7	G^7	C A^7	D^7 G^7

or this turnaround using *tritone substitutions:*

I / ♭III^7 /	II^7 / ♭II^7
C E♭^{7}	D^7 D♭^{7}

2. Honkytonk flavor with diminished seventh chords

I / I^7 /	IV / #iv°7 /	I / iv^{m6} /	I°7 / I^7 /
C C^7	F F#°7	C F^{m6}	C°7 C^7
IV / / /	#iv°7 / / /	I / i°7 /	iv^{m6} / I /
F	F#°7	C C°7	F^{m6} C
IV / #iv°7 /	I^6 / VI^7 /	II^7 / V^7 /	I^6 / V^7 /
F F#°7	C^6 A^7	D^7 G^7	C^6 G^7

Notice that diminished seventh chords always serve a ***"passing"*** function. That is, they pull from one chord to another.

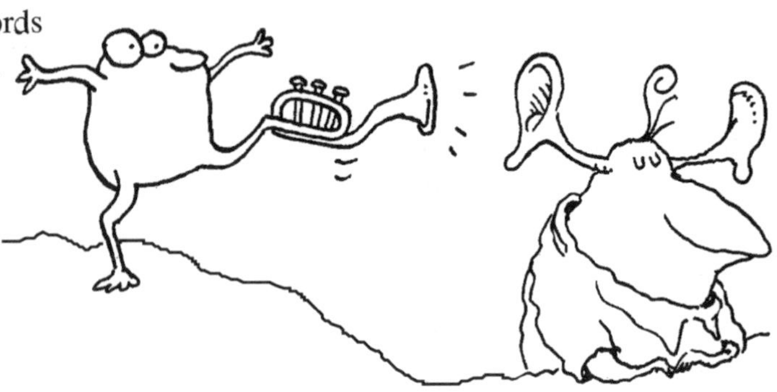

3. With major sevenths and modulating two-fives

I^{M7} / / /	$vii^{m7\flat5}$ / III^{7} /	vi^{m7} / II^{7} /	v^{m7} / I^{7} /
C^{M7}	$B^{m7\flat5}$ E^{7}	A^{m7} D^{7}	G^{m7} C^{7}
IV^{M7} / / /	$\#iv^{m7\flat5}$ / VII^{7} /	iii^{m7} / / /	$iii^{m7\flat5}$ / V^{7} /
Fmaj7	$F\#^{m7\flat5}$ B^{7}	E^{m7}	$E^{m7\flat5}$ A^{7}
ii^{m7} / iii^{m7} /	IV^{6} / V^{13} /	iii^{m7} / V^{7} /	$ii^{m7\flat5}$ / V^{7} /
D^{m7} E^{m7}	F^{6} G^{13}	E^{m7} A^{7}	$D^{m7\flat5}$ G^{7}

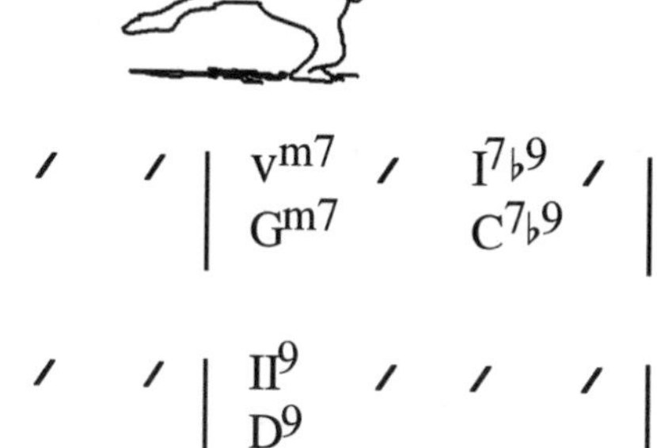

4. Relative minor flip-flop with modulating two-fives

vi^{m7} / / /	$viii^{m7\flat5}$ / $\flat VII^{7}$ /	vi^{m7} / / /	v^{m7} / $I^{7\flat9}$ /
A^{m7}	$B^{m7\flat5}$ $B\flat^{7}$	A^{m7}	G^{m7} $C^{7\flat9}$
IV^{6} / / /	iv^{m7} / $\flat VII^{7}$ /	vi^{m7} / / /	II^{9} / / /
F^{6}	F^{m7} $B\flat^{7}$	A^{m7}	D^{9}
ii^{m7} / / /	iv^{m7} / $\flat VII^{7}$ /	I / / /	$vii^{m7\flat5}$ / III^{7} /
D^{m7}	F^{m7} $B\flat^{7}$	C	$B^{m7\flat5}$ E^{7}

5. Mongrel: (debatably) Phrygian flavored (also try using add 9ths, etc.)

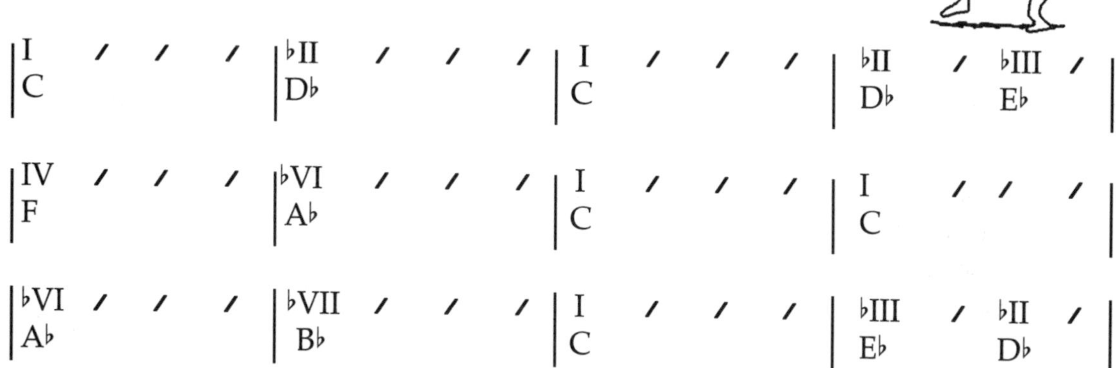

I / / /	♭II / / /	I / / /	♭II / ♭III /
C	D♭	C	D♭ E♭
IV / / /	♭VI / / /	I / / /	I / / /
F	A♭	C	C
♭VI / / /	♭VII / / /	I / / /	♭III / ♭II /
A♭	B♭	C	E♭ D♭

This last one would probably make (and indeed *has definitely made*) any self-respecting blues aficionado cringe, and is only included to give you an idea of one direction that could be taken with the twelve bar blues format. Your imagination is the limit!

Chapter 28~ Some Other Common Song Forms

What: The fact is, most songs or pieces fit into some kind of *form*.

Why strive to understand common song forms? Yet another wonderful question! If you know the common song forms and their tendencies, you will immediately be *much* farther along in being able to understand and play *any* song. You've found by now, I trust, that understanding scales and chords allows you to make sense of otherwise seemingly random notes. The same holds true for phrases that make up the sections that make up songs. Whether you are consciously aware of it or not, there are often very predictable patterns recurring in the songs you listen to and play. Being consciously aware of these patterns makes learning them that much easier. This will also be very helpful in figuring out songs by ear; covered in chapter 30.

Song Anatomy 101

Here are some of the important parts of songs that your ear already knows. Let's make sure your brain does too. Think of these as commonly true general descriptions—there are always exceptions… thankfully! Further, not all songs have all of these sections.

Introduction: an intro can serve to "set up" the song, framing what is to come.

Verse: the ***verse*** generally appears repeatedly, with *the same melody* (or a slight variation), but *different words* each time.

Chorus: the chorus also generally appears repeatedly, but both the melody and the words are the same each time. It's the part of the song everyone seems to know best. In fact, in the case of older songs—especially from the turn of the century and some decades thereafter, the chorus is often the only part which people still know and perform. The word is also used, confusingly, to refer to one complete repetition of the whole song form. For example, once through the AABA form would be one chorus.

Refrain: a refrain also recurs with the same melody and words each time, but is shorter than a chorus— often one line, or even just a few words. Songs with refrains are especially common in many folk musics. Examples of songs with refrains are *Camptown Races, Old MacDonald,* many sing-alongs, and many, many Irish songs.

Bridge: the bridge is the section which "goes away," and does something different from the verse and chorus. It is often in a different key than the rest of the song. A bridge can be a whole section, or just a phrase as in the case of the "AABA" form. Not all songs have bridges.

Break: often used interchangeably with *bridge*, a break can also be a short (often instrumental) interlude. Not all songs have breaks.

Tag: a tag is a line or two which comes after a longer section, and may be a variation of the previous material. The variation may be in instrumentation, melody, and/or harmony.

Solo: probably self-explanatory, many songs have a section where an instrument improvises a solo. More often than not, the chords under the solo are those of the verse, chorus, or bridge. More rarely, the chords under the solo are unique to the solo section itself.

Coda: a coda (Italian for *tail)* is the "end bit." A coda can be as short as a measure, or even longer than the verse and chorus. A coda often just emphasizes the tonic chord, or sometimes makes the listener long for that final tonic chord by using chords that prolong the dominant, or a dominant substitute.

Phrases: first of all, expect to find mostly phrases consisting of even numbers of bars—usually four—in most types of music. This seemingly grandiose and sweeping generalization is so often true, it justifies the seemingly grandiose and sweeping generalization. Interesting exceptions often occur in folk songs—especially Celtic—that tell stories. This may seem like a strange distinction, but often, in story songs with many, many verses, an extra bar or two will be inserted after some or all of the phrases. In my opinion, although I can't prove it, this is to give the poor singer a chance to catch his or her breath!

I highly recommend Jack Perricone's *Songwriting Workbook* not only to budding songwriters, but to anyone wanting to understand song structure. It reads easily, and is insightful and revealing. It's available only from the Berklee College of Music book store: (800) 670-0023.

Some Common Song Forms

AABA: The 32 bar *AABA* form is extremely common, especially in the world of jazz standards—enough so that it warrants special explanation. The letters AABA refer to the *phrases of the song*, not notes or chords. Each phrase is commonly eight bars long. The first, second, and fourth phrases (A) are alike, often with small melodic changes especially at cadences, although the words will probably be different each time. The B section (often called the *bridge*) provides contrast, and is often in a different key. Several well-known AABA form songs are *Smoke Gets in Your Eyes*, *Satin Doll*, *Girl from Ipanema*. I doubt I know how to count high enough to count all the AABA songs ever written!

In AABA forms, you can expect to find certain cadences at certain points. This expectation will not be fulfilled in every case, but often you will find a half-cadence or deceptive cadence at the end of the first "A" phrase, a full cadence at the end of the second "A" phrase, often moving gradually or suddenly towards the key of the bridge. The cadence at the end of the "B" section varies widely from song to song. Finally, expect a full cadence at the end of the fourth "A" phrase. Review chapter 19.

12 Bar Blues: This important song form is introduced in chapters 9 and 27, and used as a vehicle for piano instruction in **Edly Paints the Ivories Blue**. Also look for countless variations on 12 bar blues.

ABBA: This form, found especially in folk music, consists of a phrase, a different phrase twice, then the first phrase again. "The Lily of the West" 𝄞 is a stunning example of ABBA form. One of the wonderful things about this form—which this song illustrates so well—is that the phrases swap "question" and "answer" roles. This is to the extent that on first hearing, I didn't even realize that the two **B** phrases were the same phrase! Phrases' positions in the phrase structure of a song can have *that* much of an effect! (By the way, notice that the *pickup notes*—the two eighths at the beginning, and the quarter note or two eighths at the end of each line—belong to the phrase that follows. A language analogy would be sentences that begin, "So, the dog said to the cat…" rather than, "The dog said to the cat…")

Lily of the West (ABBA Form)

AABB(CC…): In this case, the letters refer to *sections*, rather than *phrases*, as in AABA or ABBA form. (The sections contain a number of phrases—very often four—within them.) A lot of folk songs and folk dance songs use this simple form. Each section is played twice, then it's back to the top for another go, and another, until everyone's had enough, and people can clap or catch their breath.

Chapter 29~ Improvisation Ideas

What: ***Improvising*** is the act (or art) of making up music on the spot. It is a fun, expressive, rewarding, and marketable skill to be able to call your own. Here are some general tips for improvising. Take any that you find helpful, and leave the rest. Warning: you will find some of these to be thought-provokingly contradictory!

Here's a very general, but important, one for starters: ***tension and resolution***, or ***dissonance and consonance*** have been mentioned before. Here they are again! Any accomplished improviser is aware of, and is working or playing with, tension and release. An accomplished improviser also knows what chord is being played at a given moment, which notes are ***chord-tones*** for that chord, which ***nonchord-tones*** are obvious choices, and which *nonchord-tones* will fall upon the ears as more surprising.

A beginning improviser can begin this process by listening carefully to the sound of individual notes—one at a time—played over a given chord, and learning to decide for him/herself whether those notes sound resolved, or unresolved. This last point, although just one sentence, represents a long and valuable process, and is in sharp contrast to the beginner's tendency to try to play as many notes as possible when improvising.

It could be said that there are two initially divergent (but ultimately convergent) approaches to improvising on a tune. One is to ignore the melody entirely in your improvisation and just use melodic material from your own ear and head. The other is to use the song's melody as a departure point, referring to it as much or as little as you wish. Many of these suggestions apply to both approaches, but here are some which particularly apply to the "melodic paraphrasing" approach.

Improvising By Paraphrasing a Composed Melody

Begin early or late.

Break phrases into fragments and recombine the fragments.

Repeat, omit, and/or reorder phrases.

Change octave in between phrases. Change octave in the middle of phrases.

Turn a held note into many repeated notes. Turn repeated notes into a held note.

Echo phrases at the same pitch, on different octaves, and on various scale degrees.

Use chromatic and/or diatonic upper and lower neighbors (notes above and below) before and/or after melody notes.

Add a scale or arpeggio fragment before or after parts of the melody.

Improvising from Scratch

Think in terms of phrases, not a continuous flow of notes. This is partially taken care of if you play a wind instrument. If you don't, try consciously breathing as you play. Stop playing while you're breathing, as if you *were* playing a wind instrument. This also gives the listener a chance to take in each brilliant phrase you play, instead of being entirely overwhelmed by a non-stop stream of notes.

Leave space: small spaces (rests), large spaces (between phrases), or *lots* of space.

Don't leave any space (can you handle it?!).

Surprise your dog.

Use wide melodic jumps (a fourth or more) in addition to, or instead of, small steps.

Use rhythm, and repeating rhythm.

If your instrument allows, use chords and harmonized lines in addition to single notes.

Try using just a few notes, and doing a lot with them, instead of doing very little with many notes. Recombine and reinflect them. Use repeated notes. They're free.

Ask a question in one phrase, and then answer it in the next.

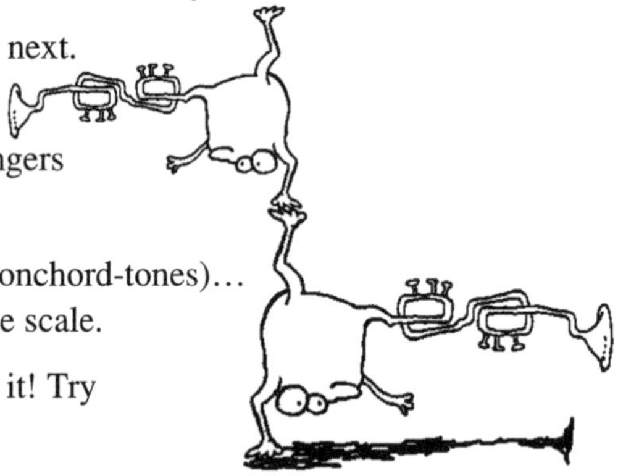

Don't curse your mistakes; use them to your advantage!! Your unconscious mind and your butterfingers are valuable sources of material!

Use only arpeggios… Then introduce passing-tones (nonchord-tones)… Then add more passing-tones until you have a complete scale.

Are you starting all your phrases on chord-tones? Stop it! Try starting on non-chord-tones for a while!

Imagine that the accompanying chords are something other than what they actually are. For example, if you're improvising over a basic blues progression, and you want to play "more outside", you could use more complex jazz substitutions as the basis for your solo.

Observe and incorporate voice-leading.

Use chromatic, rather than diatonic, passing-tones. Over a tonic major triad, natural 2, 4, 6, and 7 create a diatonic environment, while ♭2, ♯2, ♯4, ♯5, and ♯6 (or their enharmonic equivalents) create a chromatic backdrop.

Extensions (sevenths, ninths, elevenths, and thirteenths) can often be treated as chord-tones, even if they are not actually part of the chord, especially in jazzier contexts. This opens up additional possibilities, and brings a higher level of tension to the playing.

Introduce altered tones (♭3, ♯4, ♭2, etc.).

Try using upper and lower neighbor notes, either chromatic or diatonic.

Interact with the other musicians! Yes, even during *your* precious solo!

Use patterns. Superimposing a pattern onto a scale breathes new life into the scale. (Try three notes up, one down, for example.) Use a melodic pattern of a different length than the rhythmic pattern. This causes a shifting of the relationships of the two patterns.

Visual shapes (and patterns) are good idea-generators, especially on particularly visual instruments such as the string family and piano.

To get *really* left-brained, superimpose the chords in the progression to get an idea of what may be an obvious scale with which to begin. (*Obvious* doesn't necessarily always mean *best*, though.)

Another superimposition idea: if your ear is on break when you need it to tell you what you might want to play over a certain chord, this quick and dirty method is a good place to start: superimpose the notes of the chord with the notes of the key of the song (or of the blues scale, if that's the flavor you're using at the moment).

Are you thinking too much? Stop it, and try trusting your intuition. Ignore everything on this sheet for a while, kick back, and let yourself make some mistakes! Take some risks!

Are you always beginning on the same beat of the measure, on the same note, or moving in the same direction? (Many song melodies *often* do any combination of these!) Try starting on a different beat for a while, or a different beat each time you begin a phrase. And/or move in a different direction, starting from a different note.

Imagine that you're talking, and each sentence begins fine, but you forget what you're talking about by the end of every sentence. Or conversely, imagine that you are giving a speech, and you forget what your next point was supposed to be, but you barrel on anyway, and regain your focus a few words into each sentence. Now translate these two approaches onto your instrument. They can both be very liberating!

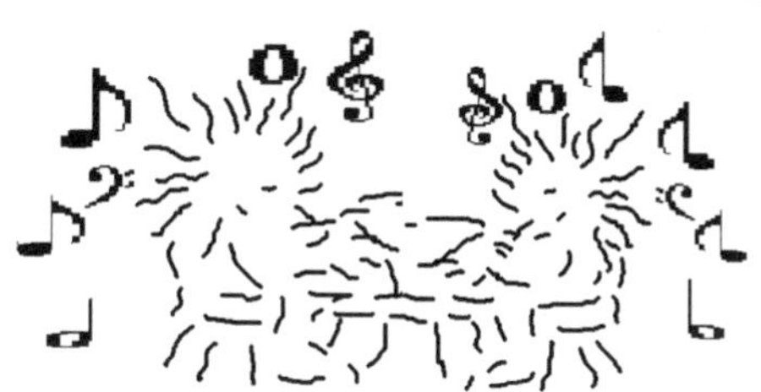

Interact with the other musicians!
Yes, even during your precious solo!!

Do you like the sound of what you're doing right at this moment? Yes? Keep doing what you're doing. No? Change to some other approach. Luckily, you're not defining a ten year policy for a multinational corporation here, you're just spinning out some melodic web from your ear, through your head, fingers, and/or your mouth. You can do it a different way tomorrow, next verse, or in two seconds! Indeed, you probably should, or else your improvisation may quickly become stale.

Use a motif (classical music talk for *riff*), or several motifs from the song's melody. This could mean tiny three or four-note phrases, or entire lines. Choose your favorite motif from the melody, and mess around with it for an entire chorus! Invert phrases, meaning if the phrase originally went up, you go down, and vice versa. Bach did it, and so can you! Displace phrases. Experiment. Use your imagination. Surprise your dog. Have fun!

Melodic phrases tend to reflect and comment on each other. Improvised phrases can often do the same. It guides the listener's ear, and brings flow to the improviser's ideas.

Don't play for a beat or two after a new chord. This gives you a chance to hear the chord and respond. This can be a life saver if you aren't sure of the chord progression—for instance if you don't *have* the sheet music to the piece. Even if you do, try this as a technique to let your ear adjust to the sound of the new chord.

Another level of freedom in improvisation involves distortion of any aspects of the song that you choose. This is easiest to implement when playing by yourself, as you can do it completely on the fly. This can include breaking the melody into smaller phrases or fragments, and inserting improvisation in between them, either symmetrically (balanced) or asymmetrically (unbalanced), or holding certain chords for extra beats or bars, changing the time or key signatures at will and inserting phrases from other songs in the middle of wherever. Maybe you want to end your solo playing a different song from the one with which you began. These approaches are bound to loosen up even the tightest player, since they require considerable fluidity and ability to respond to the moment.

Are you improvising, or regurgitating? If you have a favorite riff that seems to surface a lot, try burying it for a while! Let some new ideas come up for air! As my old friend Fred used to say, "do it new!"

Try basing an improvisation predominantly on *non-chord-tones!* Listen to the higher level of tension this imparts.

If you like a riff or phrase that you just played, play it again! Or play a variation of it. Or something contrasting. Or…

Do what sounds good to you! If it sounds good, it **is** good. Perhaps you want to ignore everything else on this page, except:

Listen! —both to yourself, **and** to anyone else with whom you're playing. This is often the hardest part of all for a beginning improviser, and is definitely one thing that separates the gems from the toys!

Add your own ideas as you think of them.

Scale/Mode Choices in Improvisation

Many people use modes to determine what notes to play over certain chords. For example, use the corresponding mode for each diatonic chord (Dorian for *iim*^{7}—specifically D Dorian for Dm^7, etc.). Alter the mode as necessary (Dorian ♭5 for a *iim*$^{7\flat5}$ for example). Or search elsewhere for another mode. For example, Locrian is a common choice for m$^{7\flat5}$ chords because the chord is diatonic to the mode: 1, ♭3, ♭5, ♭7.

Personally, I find it easier to use the major scale of the key of the song for all diatonic chords while keeping in mind what are ***chord-tones*** and what are ***passing-tones***, or ***tensions***. In the *iim*$^{7\flat5}$ example from the preceding paragraph, I would be aware that the sixth degree of the scale is lowered (appearing as the ♭5) for that chord.

A very easy way to deal with modulating two-fives and two-five-ones is to use the major scale of the key of the two-five (one), again keeping in mind the changing chord-tones. For example, in a song in the key of D, if there is a Gm^7, C^7 progression somewhere, you could use the F major scale over both of these chords, *whether or not an F chord follows.* This cuts in half the number of scales you have to think about while improvising. Now, if the Gm^7, C^7 progression is followed by a Fm chord (as opposed to F major, or something else), you could choose to use F Dorian over all three chords. This choice would give listening ears a hint of the upcoming Fm chord. *Or* you could choose to use the F major scale over the Gm^7 and C^7 chords, and switch to any of the F minor scales over the Fm chord. This choice would make the Fm chord come as more of a surprise.

This seems like a good place to mention again that *none of this is law*. These ideas are descriptions of what some musicians do, and how they might think, more than they are mandates of what **you** should do. Understanding how *others* think and do should help you on your way to deciding how *you* want to think and do.

Back to mode and scale choice. There are some chords that *do* tend to have common scales attached. One example is the *subV*^{7} chord. Lydian ♭7 mode is a common choice for this chord. The #4 of the Lydian ♭7 mode built on the ♭*II* of the scale is the ♮*V* note of the key. Got it? For example, in the key of C, the *subV*^{7} chord is D♭^{7}. D♭ Lydian ♭7 mode has a G♮ note as its raised fourth. That works well, because D♭^{7} *is* serving a substitute dominant function, after all.

There are whole books dedicated to improvisation. Seek them out if you want to be that thorough in your approach to improvising.

Again, everything I've mentioned in this section is merely intended to guide you. Once you understand these concepts (and even before), I encourage you to experiment, play from the heart as well as the mind, break any rule you can think of, etc. For example, in an overwhelmingly diatonic song, you may choose a Phrygian ♮3 scale over the one chord just because it suits your mood and ear. More power to you! Or you may choose chromatically descending melodic fragments that defy logical justification. Or you may choose to play two notes over and over again while shifting the timbre of your instrument.

Remember, the concepts in this book are jumping off points, not chains. Now go to it!

Chapter 30~ By Ear

Why: Nothing can take the place of honest to goodness ear-training. Painters learn to see colors, shapes and shading more accurately. You, as a musician, must learn to *hear* more accurately. You will then be able to play anything you hear—whether in your head, or with your ears—more quickly and easily.

What: Learn to hear music. That's a good goal, wouldn't you say? Learn to discern the sounds of different intervals, triads, modes, and rhythms. Work on your pitch memory. Pitch memory is the ability to remember and sing or play a note (or chord, or…) that you just heard—or that you heard several phrases ago.

If you own or have access to a computer, there are some excellent ear-training programs available to help you with the task. Computers are perfectly suited to teaching ear-training. They never get impatient or bored, and they're excellent at coming up with random exercises. For the Macintosh, I highly recommend Imaja's *Listen* (available at www.edly.com). I'm afraid I don't know what's currently available for Windows. But while you're getting that show on the road, here are some ideas which can make figuring out music by ear a bit easier.

If you're new to figuring out things by ear, start easy. If you can't figure out the melody to *Twinkle Twinkle* or *Silent Night*, chances are that you won't be able to figure out something more sophisticated. Go back to chapter 16 and learn to hear intervals! Learn chord progressions and become familiar with their sound, then learn to play as many songs as possible in the style(s) that interest you. Familiarity may sometimes breed contempt as it's said, but in this particular case, familiarity breeds understanding… of how a genre is put together. Then…

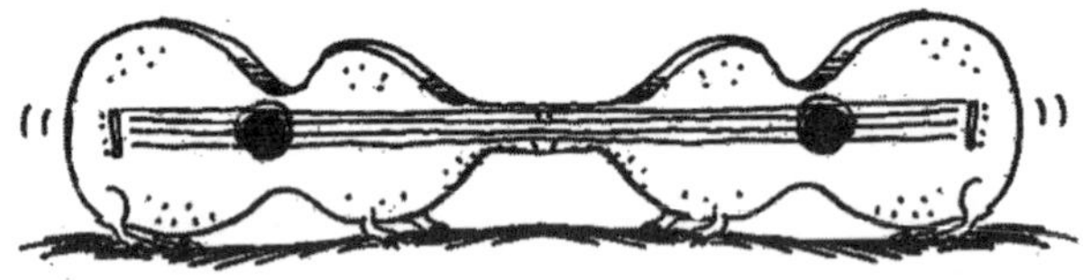

Familiarize yourself with the sound of chords moving in fifths. These progressions are one of the cornerstones of Western music. When you can hear a *V* to *I*, or a *V/V/V/V/I* (five of five of five of five… of one) progression easily, you will be much farther along than if you can't. To this end, try playing through the entire circle of fifths/fourths progression in this manner: C, C^7, F, F^7, $B\flat$, $B\flat^7$, etc.; ideally on a chordal instrument such as piano or guitar. You will find this does wonderful things for your ability to hear *V* to *I* (and similarly, *I* to *IV*) progressions.

Familiarize yourself with other standard progressions; those that make use of the ♭*VI*, such as *House of the Rising Sun*, and *Joy to the World*, or Aeolian progressions such as the last part of *Stairway to Heaven*.

Figure out what meter the song is in: is it four, three, two, or the less common compound meters of five or seven? Listen for that strong beat, which more often than not, is ONE.

Begin transcribing by notating bar lines (four per line is easy to read and follows the phrasing of most songs), repeats, key changes, etc. Start with the easiest phrases and fill in the more difficult ones later, like a crossword puzzle. This can be easier than starting at the beginning and trying to brute force your way to the end. *Also,* remember that just the melody and bass notes can give away a lot about chord alterations and qualities.

Figure out what key the song is in (many songs' verses and choruses begin and/or end on the tonic chord), including whether it's major or minor. Then figure out the melody.

Get a feel for the ***harmonic rhythm*** of the song. Is there a long time in between chord changes—eight bars, for example—or do they change very fast, perhaps every two beats? Then get more specific; try to hear *exactly* when the chords change. If you can't hear them changing, then it'll be pretty hard for you to identify what they are!

Listen for the bass notes. The bass very often plays a lot of roots, which of course gives you a big head start in figuring out the chords. Once you have the bass note, try to hear what other notes you sing or play fit with the chord. If you can figure out two notes of a chord, unless it's a fat jazz chord, chances are there aren't too many remaining!

Look for chromatically or diatonically *dropping bass lines*, common compositional techniques. Also be aware of ***pedal tones***, where the bass note stays the same while chords change above it.

Does the song use a standard song form? …12 bar blues, perhaps? …a variation thereof? (Steely Dan's "Pretzel Logic," or "Peg," and many, many things by jazz artists such as Count Basie, are examples) AABA?

Listen for the standard sections commonly found in songs.

Is the main chord progression of the song one of the common stock progressions, perhaps a *I, IV, V* progression? Bluegrass, country, some rock 'n' roll, and American folk music tend to be this way. Jazz, on the other hand, often moves through many keys in the course of a song: definitely look for modulating "two-five" progressions. Is the song circle-of-fifths-based ("Hey Joe," or "Sweet Georgia Brown," for example)? A Mixolydian approach ("Tequila," "On Broadway")? A *I, vim, IV, V* progression so popular in '50s rock ("Silhouettes")? Triads built on the notes of the minor pentatonic scale, maybe? Perhaps the "Wild Irish Rose" or "Take me out To the Ball Game" style progressions that got such widespread use around the turn of the century?

How many lines are in each section of the song? In the verse? Chorus? Are any lines repeated, or is each line different? Is part of a line used as a tag or refrain, such as is common in Irish music?

Start by looking for the *sure-to-show-up* category of chords: if you did a survey of every piece of Western music ever written, whether it be classical, jazz, rock, folk, or whatever, I'd bet my earlobes that the very most common chords would be, in order: the *I* (tonic), the *V* (the dominant), the *IV* (the subdominant), the *vim*, and perhaps then the *iim*. From there, my crystal ball begins to get hazy. This isn't just intellectual fun and games—the chords named above collectively make a good starting guess pool for novice ears and savvy seekers. I'd wager that this figures prominently in why some people "seem to know what chord is going to come next" in a jam, or when magically playing along with a song they've never heard before. They *may* have amazing ears, or they may also simply know where to look first. And knowing the right place to start your search sure speeds up the whole process, which is pretty relevant in the split-second game of responding to chord changes.

Bridges of AABA songs have several common behaviors.

1. They *very* often go immediately to, or gradually towards, the subdominant.
2. If a song is in a minor key, there's a very good chance that the bridge will be in the relative major key, or at least prominently feature the relative major chord. Also look for songs in a major key whose bridges are in the relative minor.
3. Some songs' bridges begin in a distant key and work their way back to the original key by way of secondary dominants, or perhaps just a two-five in the home key. "Smoke Gets In Your Eyes" modulates down a major third, as does Duke Ellington's "In a Sentimental Mood." The bridge in his "Sophisticated Lady" modulates down a half-step.

Coda

If you have retained even a moderate portion of this book, then you are a better musician than you were before you began reading. I would hope that most or all of what you've read will become part of your everyday musical consciousness, influencing your actions and reactions as a musician. For it's only when this kind of material is integrated sufficiently to be instantly available to your brain, fingers, and ears, that its full benefit is realized.

Actually, there's still more, if I may preach for a moment longer: I encourage you to develop your ears and your instrumental technique as much as possible. A musician with 'big ears,' a musically literate brain, and technical proficiency is a formidable one. Subtract any one of these ingredients, and you have a significantly lesser musician. But, if you add **taste**—which, as far as I know, can not be taught—to the recipe, you have a truly **outstanding** musician.

So, if this book has deepened your understanding of how music is put together, then I can consider myself successful as a teacher. If, in addition, the writing was clear and fun to read, then I can also count myself successful as an author. Finally, if what you have learned increases your **enjoyment** of music, then my time was truly well spent, and I can return, content, to my own composition and playing.

I hope this book will only be the beginning of your music study, and that you will press forward in the specific directions that interest you.

I'm going to clean up my desk now. Here's to music!

~ Edly

P.S.: I'm simmering some ideas for other books 'n' stuff. If you want to be on the **Musical EdVentures**™ mailing list for future **Edly's** releases, please e-mail me at **edly@edly.com** or write me at the address on the back cover. While you're at it, please visit my website: **http://www.edly.com**. Among many other things there, you'll find the "Ask Edly" column, where I'll answer your questions via e-mail, and post the answers, too. Tell yer friends!

Answers

Chapter 2 ~ The Major Scale

Major Scales & More Major Scales

1	2	3	4	5	6	7	(8)	♭s/#s
C	D	E	F	G	A	B	C	0
E	F#	G#	A	B	C#	D#	E	4 #s
B♭	C	D	E♭	F	G	A	B♭	2 ♭s
F	G	A	B♭	C	D	E	F	1 ♭
A	B	C#	D	E	F#	G#	A	3 #s
E♭	F	G	A♭	B♭	C	D	E♭	3 ♭s
B	C#	D#	E	F#	G#	A#	B	5 #s
G	A	B	C	D	E	F#	G	1 #
D♭	E♭	F	G♭	A♭	B♭	C	D♭	5 ♭s
A♭	B♭	C	D♭	E♭	F	G	A♭	4 ♭s
D	E	F#	G	A	B	C#	D	2 #s
F#	G#	A#	B	C#	D#	E#	F#	6 #s
G♭	A♭	B♭	C♭	D♭	E♭	F	G♭	6 ♭s
C#	D#	E#	F#	G#	A#	B#	C#	7 #s
C♭	D♭	E♭	F♭	G♭	A♭	B♭	C♭	7 ♭s

Chapter 3 ~ Major Keys and Key Signatures

Major Scales (From Fewest to Most Accidentals)

Flat Scales/Keys			Sharp Scales/Keys		
How Many Flats?	Tonic	Which Flats?	How Many Sharps?	Tonic	Which Sharps?
1 flat	F	B♭	1 sharp	G	F#
2 flats	B♭	~~B♭~~, E♭	2 sharps	D	~~F#~~, C#
3 flats	E♭	~~E♭~~, A♭, ~~B♭~~	3 sharps	A	~~C#~~, ~~F#~~, G#
4 flats	A♭	~~A♭~~, ~~B♭~~, D♭, ~~E♭~~	4 sharps	E	~~F#~~, ~~G#~~, ~~C#~~, D#
5 flats	D♭	~~D♭~~, ~~E♭~~, G♭, ~~A♭~~, ~~B♭~~	5 sharps	B	~~C#~~, ~~D#~~, ~~F#~~, ~~G#~~, A#
6 flats	G♭	~~G♭~~, ~~A♭~~, ~~B♭~~, C♭, ~~D♭~~, ~~E♭~~	6 sharps	F#	~~F#~~, ~~G#~~, ~~A#~~, ~~C#~~, ~~D#~~, E#
7 flats	C♭	~~C♭~~, ~~D♭~~, ~~E♭~~, F♭, ~~G♭~~, ~~A♭~~, ~~B♭~~	7 sharps	C#	~~C#~~, ~~D#~~, ~~E#~~, ~~F#~~, ~~G#~~, ~~A#~~, B#

Chapter 4 ~ Diatonic Intervals

The interval between each added sharp is a perfect fifth, i.e., F# up to C#. The interval between each added flat is a perfect fourth, i.e., B♭ to E♭ and E♭ to A♭. The tonic moves by perfect fifths as you add sharps, and by perfect fourths as you add flats. Yep, perfect fourths and fifths are important intervals.

Chapter 6 ~ Diatonic Harmony

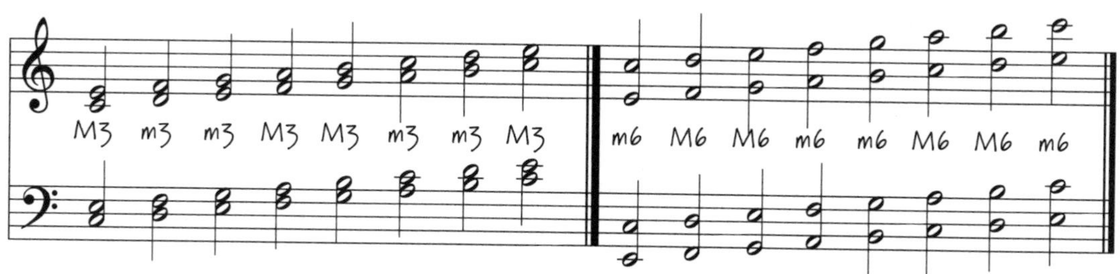

C Major Scale Harmonized in Diatonic Thirds & Sixths

Major Scale: Diatonic Harmonization In Thirds and Sixths

SCALE DEGREE:	1	2	3	4	5	6	7	(8)
Thirds:	M3	m3	m3	M3	M3	m3	m3	(M3)
Sixths:	m6	M6	M6	m6	m6	M6	M6	(m6)

The diatonic chords in the key of C: C, Dm, Em, F, G, Am, B°.

Major chords are built on the first, fourth, and fifth degrees of the major scale. Minor chords are built on the second, third, and sixth degrees of the major scale. A diminished chord is built on the seventh degree of the major scale.

The pattern of diatonic triads in all keys: *major, minor, minor, major, major, minor, diminished* … or: *I, iim, iiim, IV, V, vim, vii°*.

Chapter 11 ~ Minor Scales & Keys

More Relative Minor/Majors

G, Em	B♭, Gm	E♭, Cm	F#, D#m
B, G#m	D, Bm	A, F#m	C, Am
A♭m, C♭	E♭m, G♭	B♭m, D♭	C#m, E

Chapter 12~ The Circle of Fifths (and Fourths)

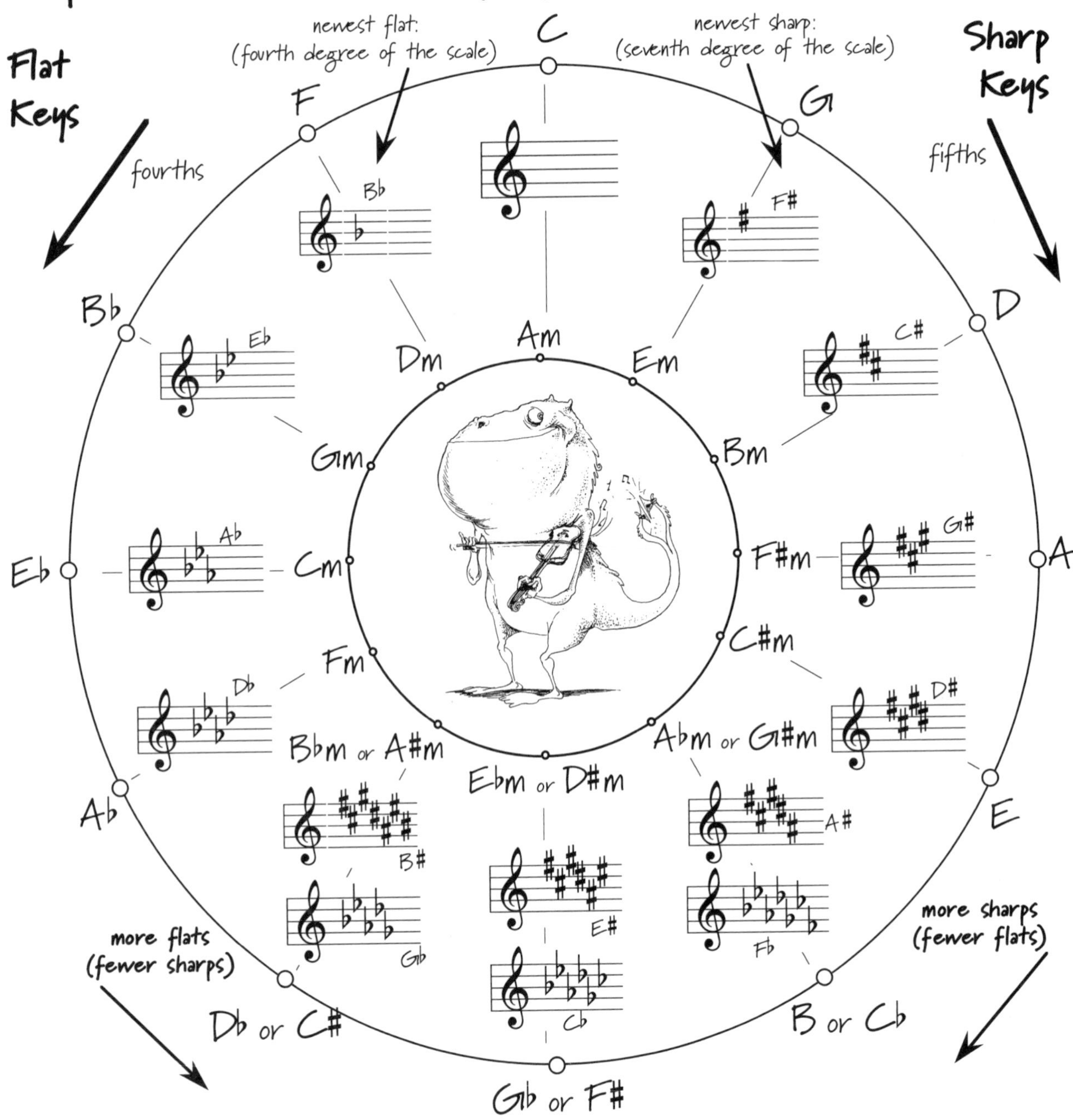

To go to the key with one more sharp or one fewer flat, ascend a P5 or go a notch clockwise. To go to the key with one more flat or fewer sharp, ascend a P4 or go a notch clockwise. The next flat to be added to a key signature will be a P4 higher (or P5 lower) than the preceding one, while the next sharp to be added will be a P5 higher (or a P4 lower). Everything on the circle moves in P4s and P5s.

Relative minors/majors are at the corresponding slot on the inner or outer ring, respectively, a M6 higher and a m3 higher, respectively.

A tonic (I or im) chord is flanked on its clockwise side by its dominant (V or vm), and on its counter-clockwise side by its subdominant (IV or ivm). Include the corresponding chords on the inner (minor) **and** outer (major) rings, and you have all of the major and minor diatonic chords of a major or minor key clustered around the tonic.

Here's a flat circle for pianists' five-finger positions: C♭, G♭, D♭, A♭, E♭, B♭, F, **C**, G, D, A, E, B, F#, C#

Chapter 13 ~ Chords: 7ths (& 6ths)

Triad, Seventh, and Sixth Chord Practice

Simpler enharmonic spellings are included where relevant.

Fmaj7..............F A C E

A♭7..................A♭ C E♭ G♭

B♭m7...............B♭ D♭ F A♭

F#.....................F# A# C#

Dm7♭5.............D F A♭ C

Em (maj7).......E G B D#

G♭.....................G♭ B♭ D♭

A+7..................A C# F G (A C# E# G)

D♭m.................D♭ F♭ A♭

Bmaj7+...........B D# G A# (B D# F× A#)

E♭m6...............E♭ G♭ B♭ C

D sus...............D G A

Cm7♭5.............C E♭ G♭ B♭

G sus...............G C D

F+.....................F A C#

D♭+..................D♭ F A

A+...................A C# F

D7...................D F# A C

Asus7..............A D E G

G°7..................G B♭ D♭ E (G B♭ D♭ F♭)

E°7..................E G B♭ D♭

B♭°7................B♭ D♭ E G (B♭ D♭ F♭ A𝄫)

D♭°7................D♭ E G B♭ (D♭ F♭ A𝄫 C𝄫)

Am7♭5............A C E♭ G

A♭m.................A♭ C♭ E♭

Dmaj7.............D F# A C#

E♭+..................E♭ G B

F#6..................F# A# C# D#

E♭m7...............E♭ G♭ B♭ D♭

AM7♭5............A C# E♭ G#

E7....................E G# B D

F7♭5................F A B E♭ (F A C♭ E♭)

F#....................F# A# C#

Dm6................D F A B

G#m................G# B D#

B♭m (maj7).....B♭ D♭ F A

C#m7♭5...........C# E G B

Chapter 14 ~ Diatonic Chords and Functions

The pattern of diatonic seventh chords:

Imaj7, iim7, iiim7, IVmaj7, V7, vim7, viim7♭5 (…or *vii*ø7, if you wish)

Chapter 21 ~ Natural Modes

Natural Modes

(half-steps are circled)

Mode Number/Name	Mode Degrees								♭s/#s
1. Ionian	1	2	3	4	5	6	7	(8)	0
2. Dorian	1	2	♭3	4	5	6	♭7	(8)	2 ♭s
3. Phrygian	1	♭2	♭3	4	5	♭6	♭7	(8)	4 ♭s
4. Lydian	1	2	3	#4	5	6	7	(8)	1 #
5. Mixolydian	1	2	3	4	5	6	♭7	(8)	1 ♭
6. Aeolian	1	2	♭3	4	5	♭6	♭7	(8)	3 ♭s
7. Locrian	1	♭2	♭3	4	♭5	♭6	♭7	(8)	5 ♭s

Modes From "Brightest" to "Darkest"

Altered Notes:	1 #	All ♮	1 ♭	2 ♭s	3 ♭s	4 ♭s	5 ♭s
Name:	Lydian	Ionian	Mixolydian	Dorian	Aeolian	Phrygian	Locrian
Degree Number:	IV	I	V	II	VI	III	VII
Tonic:	F	C	G	D	A	E	B

The pattern is tonic movement of a fifth up (or, of course, a fourth down).

Modes for true modal monsters:

E Mixolydian ......E F# G# A B C# D E

F Dorian ....F G A♭ B♭ C D E♭ F

B Locrian ....B C D E F G A B

A♭ Lydian ....A♭ B♭ C D E♭ F G A♭

D Phrygian ....D E♭ F G A B♭ C D

D♭ Aeolian...........D♭ E♭ F♭ G♭ A♭ B𝄫 C♭ D♭

F Phrygian ....F G♭ A♭ B♭ C D♭ E♭ F

B♭ Ionian ....B♭ C D E♭ F G A B♭

E♭ Lydian ....E♭ F G A B♭ C D E♭

F# Locrian ....F# G A B C D E F#

B Mixolydian ......B C# D# E F# G# A B

B♭ Ionian ....B♭ C D E♭ F G A B♭

A Dorian ....A B C D E F# G A

E♭ Lydian ....E♭ F G A B♭ C D E♭

G Aeolian ....G A B♭ C D E♭ F G

D♭ Ionian.............D♭ E♭ F G♭ A♭ B♭ C D♭

C Locrian ....C D♭ E♭ F G♭ A♭ B♭ C

E♭ Dorian.............E♭ F G♭ A♭ B♭ C D♭ E♭

E Lydian ....E F# G# A# B C# D# E

F# Aeolian...........F# G# A B C# D E F#

A Locrian ....A B♭ C D E♭ F G A

B♭ Phrygian.........B♭ C♭ D♭ E♭ F G♭ A♭ B♭

D♭ Lydian ....D♭ E♭ F G A♭ B♭ C D♭

Chapter 22 ~ Pentatonic and Blues Scales

C blues........................C E♭ F F# G B♭ C
F# blues......................F# A B C C# E F#
B♭ harmonic minor......B♭ C D♭ E♭ F G♭ A B♭
G blues ....G B♭ C C# D F G
F natural minor............F G A♭ B♭ C D♭ E♭ F
D blues ....D F G G# A C D
A♭ melodic minor........A♭ B♭ C♭ D♭ E♭ F G A♭
A♭ G♭ F♭ E♭ D♭ C♭ B♭ A♭
F blues.........................F A♭ B♭ B♮ C E♭ F
E♭ melodic minor ....E♭ F G♭ A♭ B♭ C D E♭
E♭ D♭ C♭ B♭ A♭ G♭ F E♭
B melodic minor..........B C# D E F# G# A# B
B A G F# E D C# B

B♭ blues.......................B♭ D♭ E♭ E♮ F A♭ B♭
E natural minor...........E F# G A B C D E
F natural minor ....F G A♭ B♭ C D♭ E♭ F
F# harmonic minor......F# G# A B C# D E# F#
D♭ major pentatonic ....D♭ E♭ F A♭ B♭ D♭
D minor pentatonic......D F G A C D
F major pentatonic.......F G A C D F
A major pentatonic ......A B C# E F# A
E♭ minor pentatonic.....E♭ G♭ A♭ B♭ D♭ E♭
G♭ major pentatonic ....G♭ A♭ B♭ D♭ E♭ G♭
A blues.........................A C D D# E G A
C# blues.......................C# E F# G G# B C#
G harmonic minor.......G A B♭ C D E♭ F# G

E♭ minor pentatonic and G♭ major pentatonic consist of the same notes, as do D minor pentatonic and F major pentatonic. You can also be your very own answer key by comparing, for example, the E and F natural minor scales (found one after the other for your comparing ease). The notes in each scale should be a half-step away from the corresponding notes in the other scale.

Chapter 24 ~ Chords: 9ths, 11ths, and 13ths

The pattern of diatonic ninth chords is *Imaj9, iim9, iiim7♭9, IVmaj9, V9, vim9, viim7♭5♭9*; but don't hold your breath waiting to see a *m7♭9* or *m7♭5♭9* built on *any* root.

Chapter 25 ~ Chords: Summary and Exceptions

F7#9..................F A C E♭ G#
F#/Em ....E G B F# A# C#
A♭m11 ....A♭ C♭ E♭ G♭ B♭ D♭
D♭9#11.............D♭ F A♭ C♭ E♭ G
G13 (no 11) ......G B (D) F A E
B♭m6/9.............B♭ D♭ F G C
Bmaj9#11 ....B D# F# A# C# E#
Em (maj9) ....E G B D# F#
A°7 (add 9).......A C E♭ G♭ B
Fm6/9 ....F A♭ C D G
F/E♭m ....E♭ G♭ B♭ F A C
A♭ #11 ....A♭ C E♭ G♭ B♭ D
Dm11 ....D F A C E G
E♭m13...............E♭ G♭ B♭ D♭ F A♭ C
B° ....B D F
E♭maj9#11 ....E♭ G B♭ D F A
F#maj9..............F# A# C# E# G#
C#°7 (add 9) .....C# E G B♭ D#

E♭7♭5♭9 ....E♭ G B𝄫 D♭ F♭
Am/F# ....F# A C E
Fm9♭5 ....F A♭ C♭ E♭ G
Gm9#11.............G B♭ D F A C#
A♭+9..................A♭ C E G♭ B♭
F#m7♭5..............F# A C E
C#9♭5 ....C# E# G B D#
E♭+7♭9#11..........E♭ G B D♭ F♭ A
Fm11 ....F A♭ C E♭ G B♭
E♭m7♭5...............E♭ G♭ A D♭
A♭m9/F ....F bass... A♭ C♭ E♭ G♭ B♭
F#9+...................F# A# D E G#
Cm13#11 ....C E♭ G B♭ D F# A
A7♭9...................A C# E G B♭
Fm9♭5 ....F A♭ C♭ E♭ G
F#sus9♭5.............F# B C E G#
G+7#9#11...........G B D# F A# C#
Fm11♭5...............F A♭ C♭ E♭ G B♭

Glossary and Index

I've combined the glossary and index into one handy section for all you definition seekers… all in one place, neat and tidy. Index entries are in normal type. Glossary entries are in ***bold italics***. They are quickie definitions. For more extensive definitions, refer to the main text. If you're *still* not satisfied, visit your local music store, teacher, or friendly neighborhood library. Or, be really modern and check the 'net.

C

D

diatonic chords and functions: 54

diatonic degrees: 24

diatonic intervals: 15–17

diatonic seventh chords: 54

diatonic thirds: 21–22

diatonic triads: 23,25

diminished seventh chord: 48, 51–53: a four-note chord made of stacked minor thirds: 1, ♭3, ♭5, 𝄫7 (= 6), (8).

diminished triad: 18: a ***triad*** consisting of 1, ♭3, and ♭5.

diminished interval: 29–30: a perfect or minor interval with the top note lowered a half-step.

diminished scale: 99–102: a scale made entirely of either alternating whole-steps and half-steps, or alternating half-steps and whole-steps.

dissonant; dissonance: 36, 64, 122: *tension* or *instability* (as opposed to consonance, which is *resolution* or *stability*) dissonance and consonance are fundamental motivating aspects of music. A chord which by itself might strike you as nasty might seem beautifully tense (dissonant), dying to resolve to a more consonant chord—given the right context. Music without tension can quickly become boring. Music with a lot of tension can be difficult to relax into, and tends to be an acquired taste. My favorite analogy is this: how much we like or dislike certain music is largely due to a balance between *comfort* and *surprise*. *Comfort* is having some idea of what to expect next. (Think of your favorite lullaby; it's probably not too full of big surprises!) Too much comfort, and the listener is likely to lose interest. *Surprise* keeps you on your toes, but too much of it can put the listener on edge, and *voilà*, the listener doesn't "like" the music. see also ***consonant***

dominant: 24, 31–37, 42, 48–49, 55, 57, 64–71, 78–81: the fifth ***degree*** of a scale. the chord built on the fifth degree of the scale; the dominant chord (*V*) is just *dying* to resolve back to the tonic. It is homesickness, restlessness, tension, and expectation—like a wound-up spring.

dominant chord function in minor keys: 54

dominant (*V*) chord (and chord family): 55

double flat (𝄫)***:*** iv, 8: lowers the pitch of a note by a whole-step. See also accidental.

double sharp (𝄪)***:*** iv, 8: raises the pitch of a note by a whole-step. See also accidental.

doubled: 28: duplicated

Dorian mode: 82–88, 91, 115, 126: the ***natural mode*** beginning on the second ***degree*** of the major scale; also a minor scale made by lowering the third and seventh notes of a major scale a half-step: 1, 2, ♭3, 4, 5, 6, ♭7, (8).

ear-training methods: 64

ear-training: is especially important if you want to improvise, compose, or figure out melodies and chords to songs by ear. *A good musical ear is an acquired skill, not a gift!* And like other skills, it is acquired through practice.

ear-training, intervals for: 62–65

Edly Paints the Ivories Blue**:** check it out at **http://www.edly.com**

eleventh chords: 106

enharmonic: 4–8, 30: different names for the same note—A♯ and B♭, for example. Analogous to *homonym* in grammar—enharmonics sound the same, yet are spelled differently.

extension: 49, 104–110: a chord larger than a triad; extensions include sevenths, ninths, elevenths, and thirteenths.

F & G

flat (♭)***:*** iv, 1: lowers the pitch of a note by a half-step. See also accidental.

gig: musicians' slang for a (hopefully paid) musical engagement.

guitar fretboard: 2

M

N

natural (♮)***:*** 1: cancels out a flat or sharp. See also ***accidental***.

natural minor scale: 39–41: a minor scale made up of the notes of a major scale beginning and ending on the sixth; a major scale with lowered third, sixth, and seventh degrees (♭3, ♭6, ♭7); the tonal name for Aeolian mode.

neighbor, lower *or* ***upper:*** see ***lower neighbor*** or ***upper neighbor***.

newest flat: 11: the last flat added to a flat key's key signature; the fourth degree of a major scale containing flats.

newest sharp: 11: the last sharp added to a sharp key's key signature; the seventh degree of a major scale containing sharps.

ninth chords: 104

nonchord-tone: 122: any note not in the chord.

nondiatonic: a note or chord from outside the key.

non-key-specific thinking: 74, 116: thinking in terms of how the chords of a chord progression (or notes of a melody) relate to *each other* and therefore a *theoretical tonic*—which would be the same in any key—rather than what notes make up the chord (or melody)—which would change if the example were transposed. For example: *I, iiim, IV, V*, instead of G, Bm, C, D.

O

octave: 1: (8ve) the distance from a note to the next higher or lower occurrence of that note, for example A to A, or E♭ to E♭; two notes whose vibrations are in a ratio of 2:1. "8va" means "play an octave higher."

"Oh, Susannah": the popular Stephen Foster song used in examples throughout this book.

"Old MacDonald": 31-32

"one-four-five" progression: see *I, IV, V* progression.

P

parallel major: 41–42: a minor scale's *parallel major* is the *major key* (or *scale*) beginning on the *same note.*

parallel minor: 41–42: a major scale's *parallel minor* is the *minor key* (or *natural minor scale*) beginning on the *same note.*

passing chord: 20, 52–53: a chord that pulls from a preceding chord to a following chord. Passing chords tend to be *unstable.*

passing-tone: 126: a note between two ***chord-tones*** in a melody or chord progression; a ***non-chord-tone***; they *tend* to fall on weak parts of beats ("off-beats") or weak beats in a bar (beats two and four in a meter of four, or beats two and three in a meter of three); they tend to be the *same length* or *shorter* than other melody notes.

pedal tone: 128: a long bass note which is held while chords continue to change above it

pentatonic scale: 94, 99: any five note scale; see also ***minor pentatonic scale*** and ***major pentatonic scale***.

perfect interval: 16–17, 30, 44, 59–61, 64, 65: perfect unison, fourth, fifth, and octave; the only interval quality which inverts to the same quality, perfect intervals invert to perfect intervals.

Phrygian mode: 82–88, 91, 115: the ***natural mode*** beginning on the third ***degree*** of the major scale, also made by lowering the second, third, sixth, and seventh notes of a major scale a half-step each: 1, ♭2, ♭3, 4, 5, ♭6, ♭7, (8).

piano keyboard: 2

pitch: how *high* or *low* a note is.

pivot chord: 71: a chord that acts as a transition between two keys; often V^7 of the new key.

polychord: 109–110: two chords superimposed: one chord voiced above another. Sometimes it's easier to name large chords as polychords.

Q & R

quality, chord: see ***chord quality***.

quality, interval: see ***interval quality***.

refrain: 119

relative major: 39, 40–42, 58, 94, 129: a minor chord or scale's relative major is the major chord or scale built on the note a minor third higher.

relative minor: 39, 40–42, 58, 94, 129: a major chord or scale's relative minor is the minor chord or scale built on the note a major sixth higher.

root: the note a chord is built upon; also sometimes used informally instead of ***tonic***—the first (and last) note of a scale.

root position: 26–28: the ***inversion*** where the root is the lowest note in the chord—the remaining notes are stacked above.

rhythm: patterns formed by the succession of long and short notes

S

Scale/Mode Choices in Improvisation: 126

scale: 3–11, 39–43, 82–102, 126: a melodic arrangement of notes in a specific ascending and descending order, encompassing one or more octaves. The pattern determines the scale type. There are many types of scales.

scale degree: see ***degree, scale***

Secondary Dominants and Other Secondary Chords: 65–71

secondary dominant: a major chord or dominant seventh (or an extension) that pulls to its respective (major or minor) tonic, when that tonic is a chord *other than* the tonic of the key.

seventh chords: 48–53

sharp (#)***:*** iv, vi, 1, 2, 4, 7, 8: raises the pitch of a note by a half-step. See also accidental.

sight-singing: 16: singing from musical notation, especially without prior rehearsal.

sixth chords: 48–53: four-note chords in which the *sixth* of the scale rather than the *seventh* or *lowered seventh* is added (sixth: 1, 3, 5, 6; and minor sixth: 1, ♭3, 5, 6). These chords are exceptions to the rule of forming chords by stacking thirds.

Song Anatomy 101: 119

song form: 33–34, 119–121: the skeleton of a song upon which niceties such as melody, harmony, rhythm, lyrics, and arrangement are hung.

staff: the five lines upon which music is notated.

subdominant: 24, 31–38, 44, 55–58, 78: the fourth degree of a scale; the (major) chord built upon that note (*IV*). role of: 56

submediant: 24, 36–38, 55–58, 78: the sixth degree of a scale; the (minor) chord built upon that note (*vim*). role of: 56

sub iim^7 ***chord:*** 81: a minor seventh chord (which can be extended and/or chromatically altered) built on the lowered sixth degree of a scale (♭vim^7), a ***tritone*** away from the *iim* chord. The name comes from the fact that, in jazz, this chord is often substituted for the iim^7 chord.

subV^7 ***chord:*** 79–81: a dominant seventh chord (which can be extended and/or chromatically altered) built on the lowered second degree of a scale (♭*II*)—a ***tritone*** away from the *V* chord. The name comes from the fact that, in jazz, this chord is often substituted for the V^7 chord.

subtonic: see ***leading tone***

suffix, chord: 18, 73, 113: the *quality* or *type* of chord, for example: major, m^7, $+^{7\#9}$, etc.

supertonic: 24, 56, 66, 113: the second degree of a scale; the minor chord built upon it (*iim*).

"Sweet Georgia Brown": 68, 128: a popular song; an example of multiple secondary dominants.

symmetrical chords (and functions of): 51: a chord that is made up of only one type of interval; for example, the augmented triad (+) consists of stacked major thirds (1, 3, #5, 8), and the diminished seventh chord (°7) consists of stacked minor thirds (1, ♭3, ♭5, 𝄫7 (=6), 8).

T

tempo: the speed of the beat, most accurately and commonly described in *beats per minute*.

tensions: 98, 126: (jazz term) notes added to a seventh chord to add further tension to the chord, including ♭5, +5, ♭9, 9, ♯9, 11, ♯11, and 13.

tetrachord: the first or last four notes of a scale; also, informally, a four-note (7th or 6th) chord: 48,–53, 54–55, 57.

thirteenth chords: 80, 107

tonic: 2, 10, 23, 24, 31: the first ***degree*** of a scale and the chord family (including extensions, especially sevenths and ninths) built on it.

tonic (I) chord family: 55

transposing instruments: 74

transposition: 72–75: changing a melody or chord progression from one key to another. The relationships *between the notes* stay the same, but the notes themselves are all different.

triad: 18–20, 23–25: the simplest type of chord: three notes built of stacked thirds; the first, third, and fifth notes of a major scale, chromatically altered depending on chord type.

tritone: iv, 29, 52, 55, 80, 101, 102: an ***interval*** of three (tri-) ***whole-steps***; a diminished fifth or augmented fourth.

tritone substitution: 79–81: substituting the ***sub**V^7* chord (the dominant seventh, which can also be extended and chromatically altered, built on *♭II*), for the V^7 chord; a common jazz reharmonization technique.

turnaround: 34, 35, 117: a *V* chord (and often several chords preceding) in the last bar (or two) of a blues progression. Turnarounds propel the listener (and players) back to the top for another go. Turnarounds also usually involve some kind of rhythmic or textural variation.

twelve bar blues: 33–35, 116–118: an extremely common and important song form lasting twelve measures, and, in its simplest form, using only (or mostly) the *I, IV*, and *V* chords.

two-five: 56, 67–68, 118, 126, 128–129: a progression of two chords: *iim, V*; and including extensions and chromatic alterations such as iim^7, V^7 or $iim^{9\flat5}$, $V^{7\flat9}$. Considered the most important chord progression in jazz.

two-five-one: 56, 67–68, 118, 126, 128–129: a ***two-five*** progression followed by the ***tonic*** chord: *iim, V, I*, or iim^7, V^7, I^6, for example.

U & V

upper neighbor: 122, 124: a note diatonically above another note (diatonic upper neighbor) or chromatically above another note (chromatic upper neighbor).

verse: 119: the section of a song that generally appears repeatedly, with *the same melody* (or a slight variation), but *different words* each time.

voicing: 49, 105, 110: the inversion and spacing of a chord.

voice-leading: 27, 28, 123: making transitions between chords as smooth as possible by treating chords as if each note in each chord were sung by a different singer or instrument, and using common tones where possible.

W & X

whole-step/half-step diminished scale: 100: module of alternating whole-steps and half-steps

whole-tone (whole-step) ***scale:*** 101: a scale made of only whole-steps.

whole-step: 1: an interval of two half-steps.

Y & Z

your cousin Alice: 39

2002/10/14 11:41:45 2002/10/10 11:01:55

0966161602

bill simpson

(502) 969 – 2878

11-17

Edly's Music Theory for Practical People by Ed Roseman; Peter Reynolds

9954209788272@booksamillioninc.com

SX

10-17

LM on machine

BAM – 586

586-2342643068681

586 – 2342643068681

$25.00 – ncom126

BAM!

Store # 586

992 Breckenridge Lane

Louisville KY 40207

502-894-8606

Description	QTY	PRI	TAL
001656265 EDLY	1	$22.	$22.50
Original Pr			
Primary DC		$5.00	$5.00
12			

Sub Total	$27.50
Tax 0.00	$1.35
al	$28.85

MasterCard Credit Card $28.85

Acct# 542358592047-XXXX Auth# 001635

You could buy it some place else,

But why pay more?

Save 10% with your discount card!

Millionaire Club Savings - $2.50

Associate:JULIE ID: 8758

Trx 9641 Str 586 Reg 01 Till:34 10/21/02 13:29

Want to be notified of future **Edly's** releases from **Musical EdVentures™**? E-mail me at **edly@edly.com** or drop me a note at the address below and I'll put you on my snail- or e-mailing list. Think of this as a registration card that you don't have to cut out.

Also, visit my website: **http://www.edly.com**, where, among other things, you'll find the "Ask Edly" column, a forum for theory and other music-related questions.

Other **Edly** items available from **Musical EdVentures™**:

Books:

- **Edly Paints the Ivories Blue** book 1 (ISBN 0-9661616-8-8, $12)
  Hip and fun piano instruction using the blues. This book teaches piano technique, reading skills, improvisation, chords, and related theory using blues songs written specifically for piano instruction. It is intended for lovers of blues, jazz, rock, or any pop styles, as well as "recovering traditionally-trained players." Bypassing twinkling stars and little lambs, *Edly Paints the Ivories Blue* is a bright blue alternative and supplement to traditional black & white major scale-based piano instruction books.

Original Compositions:

- A growing selection of my eclectic music—basic to advanced—from delicate to grandiose, serene to raucous, and ethereal to outrageous—for band, string and full orchestra, jazz ensemble, and various chamber ensembles. Sample scores and recordings are available at www.edly.com. Check 'em out!

Music Software:

- **Listen**: This excellent Macintosh ear-training software by Imaja's Greg Jalbert is a great companion to the book you're holding. I've used this software for years and can vouch for its effectiveness. It's entirely configurable and, therefore, good for novices through professionals.

Furthers:

- Visit www.edly.com for samples, or get in touch for more info.

Musical EdVentures™
106 Arundel Road • Kennebunkport, ME 04046
(207) 967-5433 • fax: (419) 818-4688
http://www.edly.com e-mail: edly@edly.com